REPORT

Managing Air Force Joint Expeditionary Taskings in an Uncertain Environment

John A. Ausink, Cynthia R. Cook,
Perry Shameem Firoz, John G. Drew,
Dahlia S. Lichter

Prepared for the United States Air Force

PROJECT AIR FORCE

The research described in this report was sponsored by the United States Air Force under Contract FA7014-06-C-0001. Further information may be obtained from the Strategic Planning Division, Directorate of Plans, Hq USAF.

Library of Congress Cataloging-in-Publication Data

Managing Air Force joint expeditionary taskings in an uncertain environment / John A. Ausink ... [et al.].
    p. cm.
  Includes bibliographical references.
  ISBN 978-0-8330-4947-6 (pbk. : alk. paper)
  1. United States. Air Force—Operational readiness. 2. United States. Air Force—Organization. 3. Unified operations (Military science) I. Ausink, John A.

  UG633.M296 2011
  358.4'1460973—dc22

                                                                                        2010039496

The RAND Corporation is a nonprofit institution that helps improve policy and decisionmaking through research and analysis. RAND's publications do not necessarily reflect the opinions of its research clients and sponsors.

RAND® is a registered trademark.

Published 2011 by the RAND Corporation
1776 Main Street, P.O. Box 2138, Santa Monica, CA 90407-2138
1200 South Hayes Street, Arlington, VA 22202-5050
4570 Fifth Avenue, Suite 600, Pittsburgh, PA 15213-2665
RAND URL: http://www.rand.org/
To order RAND documents or to obtain additional information, contact
Distribution Services: Telephone: (310) 451-7002;
Fax: (310) 451-6915; Email: order@rand.org

Preface

The U.S. Air Force has been operating in the U.S. Central Command (USCENTCOM) area of responsibility (AOR) since 1990, supporting both service-specific and joint taskings. Since 2004, Air Force involvement has also included "joint sourcing solutions": providing needed personnel in situations in which the traditional force provider does not have the capacity to satisfy a force capability. This study arose from concerns that demands placed on the Air Force by joint sourcing solution requirements would affect the Air Force's ability to fulfill its agile combat support role in other areas. The Air Force's Director of Resource Integration, Deputy Chief of Staff for Logistics, Installations, and Mission Support, Headquarters U.S. Air Force (AF/A4/7P), asked RAND Project AIR FORCE to help the Air Force develop a methodology to measure the effect of joint taskings on agile combat support capabilities and explore ways for the Air Force to better accommodate demands for these taskings.

This report documents the results of RAND's research in this area and describes two new tools that, using currently available data, can help the Air Force forecast the impact of joint sourcing solutions (and other deployment demands) on the deployment availability of individual career fields and on the combat capability of the Air Expeditionary Force (AEF).

The research reported here was sponsored by AF/A4/7P and conducted within the Resource Management Program of RAND Project AIR FORCE for a fiscal year (FY) 2008 study "Understanding the Effects of Joint Taskings on Air Force Agile Combat Support Capabilities." It should be of interest to decisionmakers and analysts involved in determining how the deployment of Air Force personnel should be managed.

RAND Project AIR FORCE

RAND Project AIR FORCE (PAF), a division of the RAND Corporation, is the U.S. Air Force's federally funded research and development center for studies and analyses. PAF provides the Air Force with independent analyses of policy alternatives affecting the development, employment, combat readiness, and support of current and future aerospace forces. Research is conducted in four programs: Force Modernization and Employment; Manpower, Personnel, and Training; Resource Management; and Strategy and Doctrine.

Additional information about PAF is available on our website:
http://www.rand.org/paf/

Contents

Figures

Tables

Summary

In addition to providing military support to Operation Iraqi Freedom and Operation Enduring Freedom in Afghanistan through its AEF structure, the Air Force has been providing personnel since 2004 for what are called "joint sourcing solution" assignments (formerly, ILO, or "in-lieu-of" positions) in Iraq and Afghanistan. These are situations in which the "preferred provider" (usually the Army) has insufficient available personnel to meet a certain need and another military service is required to fill it. For example, a unit of Air Force civil engineers might be used to replace an Army construction engineering unit and would be assigned to an Army organization during the deployment.

By FY 2008, joint sourcing solution positions filled by Air Force personnel accounted for almost 25 percent of the 25,000 airmen located in the USCENTCOM area of operations. Air Force leadership recognizes that filling these positions is a valid combatant command (COCOM) requirement that must be met in order to accomplish the military mission. Nonetheless, because Air Force personnel have the expertise necessary to satisfy emergent requirements in nontraditional support missions, certain career fields (such as security forces and logistics readiness officers) are experiencing deployment strains well beyond what would be expected under the planned AEF construct. This study arose from AF/A4/7P concerns that demands placed on the Air Force by joint sourcing solution requirements would affect the Air Force's ability to fulfill its agile combat support role in other areas. A better understanding of the new requirements will help the Air Force make resource allocation decisions that will ensure that it can satisfy the full range of demands for its capabilities.

Process

To help determine the impact of these assignments on the Air Force, we first studied the process that links the origination of a new requirement (a request for forces, or RFF) to the assignment of the requirement to a specific service. Overall, we found that the process functioned well and was not a factor in any impact of joint sourcing assignments on the Air Force—beyond the fact that the Air Force has capabilities that the COCOM requires. A major complaint from participants in the process from all the services, however, is that requests for *forces* should instead be requests for a *capability* and that the services should be allowed more flexibility in suggesting options to meet a COCOM requirement.

Supply and Demand Analysis

Air Force personnel raised two major concerns during interviews for this study. One was the difficulty in conveying to Air Force leadership—and to their counterparts in other services and on the Joint Staff—the current impact of joint sourcing assignments on individual career fields and the limited availability of personnel in some career fields for deployment. The second was the difficulty of expressing potential future impacts of agreeing to fill joint sourcing positions. We developed three approaches for addressing these concerns.

First, we showed how currently available data collected by the Air Force Personnel Center (AFPC)/Directorate of AEF Operations (DPW) (formerly known as the AEF Center) can be used to study the cumulative impact of joint sourcing assignments on different career fields and how these data, combined with other publicly available Air Force personnel data, can be used to compare the supply and demand of personnel using various demographic categories in ways that are more illuminating than the displays that are commonly used. (See pp. 11–17.)

Second, we developed a new modeling tool that helps forecast the impact of RFFs on deployment availability over time. Some organizations already use an "availability pyramid" that starts with the total number of personnel in a given career field and then subtracts personnel in various categories who are not deployable (because of, for example, inexperience, illness, or assignment to a job that "must" be filled) in order to determine the actual number of personnel who are available to fill an emergent joint sourcing solution requirement. While these pyramids were useful, they were limited because they were snapshots of a moment in time. Our new tool extends the basic idea of the pyramid and allows an analyst or functional area manager to study the potential impact over time of fulfilling an RFF. It also allows the user to adjust various policy "levers" (such as deployment-to-dwell ratios, recruitment, and retention) in order to discern how policy changes might help balance the supply of, and demand for, deployed personnel. The tool has the potential to allow automatic updates from a centralized data source, standardizing measures of impact while allowing the flexibility for inputs that vary by career field. (See pp. 19–25.)

Third, we developed two approaches to measure the impact of joint sourcing assignments on AEF capabilities. Both approaches make use of information derived from long-term force requirements outlined in the U.S. Department of Defense's Steady State Security Posture, as well as Air Force personnel availability data from the AEF library. One approach displays potential capability shortfalls by Air Force Specialty Code (AFSC); the other displays potential shortfalls over time for a particular AFSC and takes into account the possibility that some assignments will "break" other unit type codes (UTCs)—that is, filling a joint sourcing solution might make unavailable an AFSC that is critical for a UTC that provides a completely different capability. Both tools have the potential to enhance the Air Force's ability to plan for future demands on its forces. (See pp. 25–31.)

In-Garrison Capability

One goal of this study was to develop measures of the "in-garrison" impact of joint sourcing assignments—that is, how unanticipated deployments of personnel to non-AEF positions can affect functions at a base from which the personnel are deployed. This proved difficult for several reasons. First, it is very difficult to establish standard metrics for "in-garrison performance." For example, if a small headquarters staff loses an officer to a joint sourcing assignment, the workload of those left behind would increase. A training unit would also suffer if it lost an officer instructor to a joint sourcing requirement, but it would be difficult to develop a common measure to show which organization's mission was affected more. Second, filling joint sourcing assignments can affect unit services that are not directly related to mission accomplishment. For example, if joint sourcing assignments result in a shortage of finance officers at a given base, other base personnel might be inconvenienced, but it would be difficult to measure the impact on mission accomplishment. It would also be impossible to distinguish the impact of an absence due to a joint sourcing requirement from that due to another type of absence, such as an AEF assignment. Finally, the Air Force (like the other services) tends to have a "can-do" attitude, which means that personnel will work very hard to accomplish their mission. Thus, it may not be obvious that a unit is overstressed until the loss of one more person to a deployment leads to some sort of mission failure. This breaking point is difficult to predict. (See pp. 33–39.)

Our suggestions for new ways of looking at available data and the new tools we have developed for analyzing career fields and AEF capabilities should help the Air Force better understand the potential impact of future joint sourcing requirements.

Acknowledgments

This research was sponsored by Maj Gen Polly Peyer when she was Director of Resource Integration in the Office of the Deputy Chief of Staff for Logistics, Installations and Mission Support, Headquarters U.S. Air Force (AF/A4/7P). Michele Rachie and Kathe Graham, AF/A4/7P, served as advisers. We thank them for their sponsorship and interest in this work.

During this research effort, we interviewed personnel in the Joint Staff's Office of the Deputy Director for Regional Operations (J3/DDRO), the Air Force Operations Group (which helps manage the Air Force portion of the process), the Air Force's War and Mobilization Planning Policy Division (AF/A5XW), and many other offices, but we would like to individually recognize several people who were particularly helpful.

Col James Ogden (AF/A5XJ) and CDR Kevin Meenaghan (JCS/J3/JOD) gave us excellent background briefings on the Global Force Management process. Trent Dudley (AF/A5XW) provided significant help and insights throughout this project, especially regarding the AEF Tempo Banding concept. Repeatedly, when we had difficult questions, our interviewees suggested that we talk to Trent, who always had the answers.

Maj Jenny Christian and Chris Merlo (AF/A4/7Z) highlighted Air Force–specific aspects of the joint sourcing process. Lt Col Heather Buono (AF/A4/7PE) connected us with airmen who had recently served, or were currently serving, on joint taskings. Maj Jerry Gonzalez (AF/A4RF) gave us a copy of a pyramid chart that led to the idea of a new forecasting model.

Col Ted Uchida, Lt Col Walt Shearer, and Lt Col Kari Smith (AF/A3O) and Lt Col Troy Dunn and Maj Alex Anastasiou (AF/A1PR) helped us understand the impact of joint sourcing assignments on different career fields.

Col Robert "Tiny" Lala invited us to conduct interviews at the AEF Center at Langley Air Force Base. Maj Michael Clavenna organized our visit there, and Mark Danielson developed the data set that helped us better understand joint sourcing demands.

We particularly thank the airmen we interviewed who had served or were serving in joint tasking assignments.

Finally, we thank Patrick Mills for his analysis of joint sourcing assignments on AEF capabilities, Susan Woodward for assistance with organizing the material, and our reviewers, Edward Keating and David Oaks, for making many suggestions that improved the presentation of our research.

Abbreviations

ACC	Air Combat Command
AEF	Air Expeditionary Force
AF/A1PR	Personnel Readiness Division, Headquarters U.S. Air Force
AF/A3OO	Air Force Operations Group, Headquarters U.S. Air Force
AF/A4/7P	Director of Resource Integration, Office of the Deputy Chief of Staff for Logistics, Installations, and Mission Support, Headquarters U.S. Air Force
AF/A4/7Z	Global Combat Support, Headquarters U.S. Air Force
AF/A5XJ	Joint Chiefs of Staff and National Security Council Matters Division, Headquarters U.S. Air Force
AF/A5XW	War and Mobilization Planning Policy Division, Headquarters U.S. Air Force
AFB	Air Force base
AFCENT	U.S. Air Forces Central (formerly, U.S. Central Command Air Forces)
AFI	Air Force Instruction
AFPC	Air Force Personnel Center
AFSC	Air Force Specialty Code
AOR	area of responsibility
BSP	baseline security posture
CJCS	Chairman of the Joint Chiefs of Staff
COCOM	combatant command
DCAPES	Deliberate and Crisis Action Planning and Execution Segments
DoD	U.S. Department of Defense
DPW	Directorate of Air Expeditionary Force Operations
FAM	functional area manager

FRED	Force Requirements Enhanced Database
FY	fiscal year
GFM	Global Force Management
GUI	graphical user interface
IDEAS	Interactive Demographic Analysis System
ILO	in lieu of
ISP	integrated security posture
J3/DDRO	U.S. Joint Chiefs of Staff, Joint Operations Directorate, Office of the Deputy Director for Regional Operations
J3/JOD-GFM	U.S. Joint Chiefs of Staff, Joint Operations Directorate, Global Force Management
JACO	Joint Action Coordinating Office
JESS	Joint Event Scheduling System
JOD	Joint Operations Directorate
MANFOR	Manpower Force Packaging System
MEFPAK	Manpower and Equipment Force Packaging
MOS	military occupational specialty
OEF	Operation Enduring Freedom
OIF	Operation Iraqi Freedom
OSD	Office of the Secretary of Defense
PAF	RAND Project AIR FORCE
RFF	request for forces
SDOB	Secretary of Defense Operations Book
SecDef	Secretary of Defense
SSSP	steady-state security posture
URF	unit request for forces
USCENTCOM	U.S. Central Command
USJFCOM	U.S. Joint Forces Command
UTC	unit type code

CHAPTER ONE

Introduction

Operations Enduring Freedom and Iraqi Freedom (OEF and OIF) have placed great demands on the U.S. Army; in July 2008, there were about 125,000 soldiers on the ground in Iraq and an additional 25,000 in Afghanistan.[1] Indeed, official Army documents state that in order to meet current and anticipated demands, the Army must grow by 74,000 soldiers over the next few years.[2] Some of these demands are for new missions, such as embedded training teams, for which the Army is not normally organized, and others are in areas (such as security forces) for which requirements exceed Army staffing. Since 2004, requests from the combatant commander of U.S. Central Command (USCENTCOM) to fulfill some so-called "emergent" requirements have been beyond what the "preferred provider"[3] (generally the Army but in some cases the Marine Corps) can meet, and as a result, other services have been tasked to fill them.

Since February 2004, many of these "joint sourcing" assignments have been filled by the Air Force;[4] from 2004 to 2008, Air Force requirements for these assignments increased from 1,900 to more than 6,000 positions. Some Air Force career fields—logistics readiness officers, security forces, and transportation personnel, among others—have been in especially high demand to fill joint sourcing assignments, while some Air Force personnel have found, upon arriving at their joint tasking assignment, that the position would have been better filled by someone from a different career field.

Because the impact of these requirements on individuals, units, specific career fields, combat support capabilities, and the Air Force as a whole is not well understood, the Director of Resource Integration, Deputy Chief of Staff, Logistics, Installations, and Mission Support, Headquarters U.S. Air Force (AF/A4/7P), asked RAND Project AIR FORCE (PAF) to help the Air Force develop approaches to measure these impacts, focusing on combat support capabilities, with the ultimate goal of helping the Air Force better prepare for future demands.

---

[1] JoAnne O'Bryant and Michael Waterhouse, *U.S. Forces in Iraq*, Washington, D.C.: Congressional Research Service, RS22449, updated July 24, 2008. Both numbers include active, guard, and reserve Army forces.

[2] U.S. Army, *2008 U.S. Army Posture Statement*, February 26, 2008.

[3] *Preferred provider* is the term used for the service that would typically provide the resources to meet a particular mission.

[4] Brigadier General Marke F. Gibson, "In-Lieu-of (ILO) Taskings," presentation to the Subcommittee on Readiness, Committee on Armed Services, U.S. House of Representatives, July 31, 2007.

Research Objective and Major Tasks

To help determine the impact of joint taskings on the Air Force, we divided this project into four major tasks. The first was to develop a basic "map" of the joint assignment process. Many Air Force and joint organizations are involved in the joint tasking assignment process, but it was uncertain whether any one organization had a clear understanding of how all elements of the process fit together. The goal was to follow the process from the establishment of a requirement to the selection of individuals to fulfill the requirement in order to illuminate approaches to understanding the impact that they have on combat support capabilities. To meet this goal, we interviewed personnel in the Joint Staff's Joint Operations Directorate, Office of the Deputy Director for Regional Operations (J3/DDRO); the Air Force Operations Group (which helps manage the Air Force portion of the process); the War and Mobilization Planning Policy Division, Headquarters U.S. Air Force (AF/A5XW); and others.

The second task was to study available personnel data on joint taskings and develop better ways to display the data to clarify the current impact of joint taskings on individuals, career fields, and, ultimately, combat support capability. This led us to discussions with the commander of the Air Expeditionary Force (AEF) Center at Langley Air Force Base (AFB) and with personnel in the combat operations support branch there who were experts on various AEF-related data systems.

The third task was related to the second but had a slightly different perspective. Air Force units have a responsibility to perform day-to-day duties and train for future operational taskings. There are currently no tools to measure the impact of joint sourcing assignments on day-to-day "in-garrison" operations or the ability to respond to unknown future operational demands. Using insights from the first two tasks, Office of the Secretary of Defense (OSD) planning guidance for future contingencies, and related RAND research, we considered approaches for developing metrics that will allow the Air Force to objectively determine how these assignments affect its combat support readiness in both cases.

A final task was to identify and assess options for the Air Force to better accommodate and respond to future demands for these taskings while minimizing any impact on readiness.

Organization of This Report

The next chapter of this report describes the joint sourcing "solution" process. Relevant guidance documents, offices involved, and service interactions often change. However, there is enough detail to understand some of the complexities of the process and show where and why some problems with it have arisen.

Chapter Three describes how data currently available to the Air Force can be used to better understand the current impact of joint taskings on individuals and career fields. Chapter Four enlarges the discussion to the potential future impact of joint taskings on career fields and AEF capabilities. Of key interest are two tools developed by RAND. The first model can help functional area managers (FAMs) better anticipate the impact on their career field of filling new requests for forces (RFFs). The second model helps forecast the impact of filling joint taskings on the Air Force's ability to provide the capabilities that it is expected to provide in order to satisfy broad national defense requirements.

In Chapter Five, we present insights, based on interviews we conducted as part of this research, related to other impacts of joint taskings—such as on individual training needs and on career development or promotion possibilities. This part of the analysis is qualitative rather than quantitative; one of the conclusions of our research is that it would be very difficult to attempt to create a standard measure of the in-garrison impact of filling joint sourcing positions (and deployed positions in general). Nonetheless, some common threads regarding other impacts of these assignments emerged from our interviews.

In Chapter Six, we present our conclusions and recommendations. Appendix A provides more details on the joint sourcing process, and Appendix B provides details on the career field forecasting model.

CHAPTER TWO

Process for Providing Joint Force/Capability Solutions

To provide a basic map of how a joint sourcing assignment originates and is filled, this chapter briefly describes important aspects of the Global Force Management (GFM) process and how joint force/capability solutions are developed. (Appendix A provides additional details.) After introducing some definitions and describing key organizations governing GFM, we discuss how rotational and emergent forces are provided and some difficulties that the services have with the process of satisfying RFFs. The process is complex, and, in our interviews, we found that personnel who were closely involved with some aspects of the process (RFF validation, for example) were unfamiliar with service-specific approaches to dealing with RFFs that, if known, could make the process more efficient.[1] However, efforts are under way to improve the process, and we found that, overall, the process functioned reasonably well and was not a factor in any negative impact of joint sourcing assignments on the Air Force.

Rotational Versus Emergent Force Requirements

There are two broad categories of forces that the military services provide to combatant commanders to satisfy the defense needs of the United States: rotational forces and emergent forces. Rotational forces are allocated to combatant commanders to execute continuing tasks in their area of responsibility (AOR) and are usually deployed as units (e.g., an Army brigade or aircraft in an AEF task force) for a specified period. Emergent force requirements are allocated in response to combatant command (COCOM) requests to fulfill *unforecasted* requirements within the AOR that cannot be fulfilled by redistributing forces that are already under the combatant commander's control.[2]

Until fiscal year (FY) 2008, situations in which a COCOM's request for forces to fill an emergent requirement could not be filled by the "preferred" provider but instead had to be filled by another source were called "in-lieu-of" (ILO) sourcing "solutions." For example, if a deployed Army unit needed more convoy drivers but the Army did not have the personnel to

---

[1] As our interviews about the process continued, we found that people were eager to learn more beyond their "stovepiped" function and would ask to participate in interviews with other organizations in order to learn more about how the process worked in practice, as opposed to in theory.

[2] U.S. Joint Chiefs of Staff, Joint Operations Directorate, Global Force Management Division (JCS J3/JOD-GFM), "Global Force Management," briefing, December 6, 2007.

provide them, the positions could be filled by personnel from the Air Force, Marine Corps, or Navy. There were three categories of ILO solutions:[3]

- *Joint sourcing solution:* A service provides a like capability within its core competency in place of another service's core mission. For example, Air Force civil engineers replacing an Army heavy construction engineering unit.
- *Re-mission solution:* A service uses an existing unit to perform a mission that is not within its core competency. For example, an Army artillery unit being retrained as a transportation unit.
- *Retrained ad hoc solution:* In cases in which team capabilities are required, an ad hoc unit is formed from a group of personnel who are then trained and deployed to support a COCOM requirement. Examples include provincial reconstruction teams and civil affairs teams.

In FY 2009, these definitions were changed so that "ILO" refers only to situations in which a standard force is deployed to execute missions and tasks outside its core competencies (what were formerly called "re-mission" solutions). Situations in which a service provides a capability in place of another service are called "joint force/capability" solutions. Few positions filled by the Air Force would be considered ILO assignments under the new definitions.[4]

Global Force Management and the Standardization of Force Allocation

The GFM initiative and the associated joint force provider process were established in 2004 to help standardize how organizational and force structure information is exchanged among different data systems.[5] Both rotational force requirements and emergent force requirements are determined through the GFM process, with some variations between them.

Figure 2.1 presents a broad overview of the interactions of organizations involved in the GFM process,[6] starting with a COCOM making a request for forces and capabilities (either rotational or emergent) to the Joint Staff. The Joint Staff provides strategic oversight by managing global availability and establishing priorities among competing COCOM needs; it also provides strategic risk assessment and guidance.

---

[3]   Definitions are from Air Force Instruction (AFI) 10-401, "Air Force Operations Planning and Execution," December 7, 2006. Examples are from the Joint Chiefs of Staff and National Security Council Matters Division, Headquarters U.S. Air Force (AF/A5XJ), "Joint Sourcing Primer," briefing provided to the authors on December 26, 2007.

[4]   It is important to be aware of the change in definitions. Air Force congressional testimony and Air Force media releases that refer to problems related to "ILO" assignments use the *former* definition. In fact, the Air Force has complicated the issue somewhat by introducing another term. On December 4, 2008, the Air Force Chief of Staff directed that, in order to emphasize the Air Force's "joint posture," the term *joint expeditionary tasking* would be used internally for all such assignments—joint source/capability, ad hoc, and re-missioning. See General Norton A. Schwartz, Air Force Chief of Staff, "Joint Expeditionary Tasking Term," memorandum, December 4, 2008.

[5]   Michael Ferriter and Jay Burdon, "The Success of Global Force Management and Joint Force Providing," *Joint Force Quarterly*, No. 44, 1st Quarter 2007. The website of the Office of the Under Secretary of Defense for Personnel and Readiness states that this was directed by the 2004 Joint Programming Guidance document. See Office of the Under Secretary of Defense for Personnel and Readiness, "Global Force Management (GFM)," web page, undated.

[6]   This figure and the accompanying discussion are derived from briefings received from AF/A5XJ and JCS J3/JOD-GFM.

Figure 2.1
GFM Process Overview

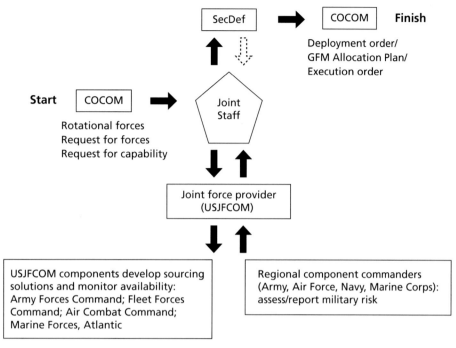

RAND *TR808-2.1*

This oversight draws on the following guidance documents:

- The Unified Command Plan, which establishes the missions, responsibilities, and force structure of the COCOMs.
- A memorandum from the Secretary of Defense (SecDef) titled "Forces for Unified Commands,"[7] which directs the peacetime assignment of forces to COCOMs and describes how execution and deployment orders are used to transfer forces between COCOMs.[8]
- The Contingency Planning Guidance provided by the Secretary of Defense to the Chairman of the Joint Chiefs of Staff (CJCS) to apportion forces to the COCOMs.[9]
- *Guidance for Employment of the Force*, an OSD document that provides guidance on priorities for force allocation.

With this guidance from the Joint Staff (represented by an arrow from the pentagon in Figure 2.1 to the "joint force provider" box), the joint force provider manages operational execution and works with the service components to develop a global joint sourcing approach,

---

[7]   The memo is an annex to the GFM document. See Ferriter and Burdon, 2007.

[8]   A deployment order is a SecDef planning directive that authorizes and directs the transfer of forces between COCOMs by reassignment or attachment. An execution order initiates military operations. See JCS J3/JOD-GFM, 2007.

[9]   U.S. Code, Title 10, Chapter 5, Sec. 153, Joint Chiefs of Staff, January 3, 2007.

identify capability and force availability concerns, and recommend sustainment actions.[10] The joint force provider components (the designated force providers of the individual services—Air Combat Command [ACC], in the case of the Air Force for USJFCOM) and regional component commanders (such as U.S. Air Forces Central [AFCENT]) manage tactical execution, developing joint sourcing solutions and assessing military risk. This interaction is represented in Figure 2.1 by the arrows to and from USJFCOM and the regional USJFCOM components. Based on this interaction, USJFCOM provides the Joint Staff with a recommended global joint sourcing solution, capability substitution options, and mobilization recommendations. As shown by the arrow from the Joint Staff to the SecDef, the CJCS recommends a solution to the SecDef,[11] and the SecDef then issues a deployment or execution order to authorize a change to the GFM Allocation Plan that will satisfy the original request from the COCOM.[12]

The GFM process makes use of the GFM Board to establish strategic-level guidance and review of force allocations before the recommendations are sent to the SecDef. The GFM Board is chaired by the director of the Joint Staff and includes representation from OSD, all COCOMs, the Joint Staff, and the individual services.[13]

Generally, the determination of requirements for rotational forces is a calendar-driven process with a series of meetings related to force allocation that are regularly scheduled throughout the fiscal year. Emergent requirements are need-driven; the same major organizations are involved, but the timeline is different and individual services may use different processes to determine their ability to satisfy them. Appendix A provides more information about how RFFs originate and are validated, as well as how the Air Force responds to them.

Problems with the Process

Discussions with action officers involved with the RFF process revealed several areas of difficulty: requests for personnel rather than capability, differences in terminology among the services, parallel staffing, and different approaches to dwell times among the services.[14] A variety of other internal Air Force staffing problems, such as lack of coordination and lack of standardization in responding to RFFs, were reported by the staffers we interviewed. However, with two exceptions (the desire for requests for capabilities instead of forces and the difficulty of translating RFFs into Air Force terminology), most of the RFF process problems were not only recognized but were in the process of being rectified.

---

[10] In Figure 2.1, the joint force provider is U.S. Joint Forces Command (USJFCOM), which is responsible for RFFs for conventional forces (as is most often the case with OIF and OEF). Requests for mobility forces go to U.S. Transportation Command, requests for special operations forces to the U.S. Special Operations Command, and requests for strategic forces/intelligence, surveillance, and reconnaissance (ISR) go to the U.S. Strategic Command.

[11] Using, if necessary, the GFM Board (described in Appendix A) to outline contentious issues of which the SecDef needs to be aware.

[12] One JCS J3/JOD-GFM staffer called the GFM Allocation Plan "a big [deployment order]." See JCS J3/JOD-GFM, 2007.

[13] JCS J3/JOD-GFM, 2007.

[14] *Dwell time, deployment-to-dwell time,* and *deployment-to-dwell ratio* refer to the time a person is deployed compared to the time the person is not deployed. A one-to-four deployment-to-dwell ratio means that if a person is deployed for one period, he or she will stay home for four periods before being deployed again. For example, if a person is deployed for four months, he or she should have 16 months at home before being deployed again.

Air Force personnel pointed out that one problem with RFFs is that they are just that: requests for forces instead of requests for capabilities.[15] In later interviews, we found that Army, Navy, and Marine Corps staffers felt the same way. Discussions with Navy personnel indicated that the Navy is particularly adept at using requests for information to better understand the capabilities required by an RFF and suggesting alternative ways to provide them. In defense of the tendency to request specific forces, when new missions arise, it can be difficult to know what type of tailored capability will be required, and requesting "standard"-sized units is an understandable fallback.

Another common difficulty involved differences in terminology among the services. For example, RFFs tend to be expressed in Army "language" (military occupational specialties, or MOSs) that is sometimes difficult to translate into Air Force classifications. For example, an "Army logistician" is different from an "Air Force logistician," and it sometimes takes the exchange of several requests for information to determine what the requirement actually is.[16] The RFF process could benefit from better translation of RFFs into the languages of the individual services.

On the Air Force side, we were told that U.S. Central Command Air Forces (redesignated as AFCENT in March 2008), for a variety of reasons, lacked the capacity—and perhaps even the expertise—to fully review RFFs as they moved through the USCENTCOM chain of command, contributing to the difficulty of translating RFFs into Air Force language.

Another problem with the RFF process is that there is sometimes "parallel staffing." When an RFF comes in, Headquarters U.S. Air Force personnel and ACC consult the same FAMs to determine whether the request can be filled. Occasionally, USJFCOM will simultaneously ask a COCOM (such as the U.S. European Command) to seek input from a component command (such as U.S. Air Forces in Europe). There have been cases in which the component command has indicated that the RFF can be filled, while Air Force headquarters (with access to more information) has determined that it cannot.[17]

Air Force staffers also felt that the Air Force is at a disadvantage in expressing the risk of approaching dwell time redlines because it determines dwell times differently from the Army. The Air Force considers dwell time from the perspective of a career field: The demand for personnel compared to the supply determines how much time personnel can spend at home before they must be deployed again. However, the Army generally deploys units instead of individuals; there are times when only a part of a unit deploys, yet the Army counts the whole unit as being deployed when determining whether it has exceeded its dwell time.[18] Air Force personnel thus feel that the risk to Army personnel or units filling an RFF is sometimes overstated when

---

[15] An RFF usually takes the form of a particular number of personnel with a recommended distribution by rank or grade. The services argue that they organize differently and that, for example, the Air Force could field a capability with a different (often lower) number of personnel.

[16] As noted in Chapter Four, the position of Army quartermaster (responsible for supply support for soldiers and units in field services, aerial delivery, and material and distribution management) represents a group of subspecialties in one of the Army's "logistics" MOSs. The Air Force does not have a corresponding officer position that requires training across this portfolio of subspecialties, so assigning an Air Force "logistics readiness officer" to a position that requires a quartermaster may not result in the right match of skills.

[17] This problem was pointed out to the Joint Staff by an Air Force action officer during one of our interviews, and a solution to the problem was suggested.

[18] This difference in approaches to determining dwell time was mentioned in an interview with Air Force FAMs in December 2007. However, we heard from sources more familiar with the Army that the Army does take into account dwell time

compared to that of other services. This discrepancy among the services will be mitigated by the Air Force's move to what it calls a "tempo-banding" concept in its AEF cycle.[19] Part of this concept involves standardizing calculations of dwell times among Air Force FAMs and paying more attention to the deployment capabilities of UTCs, which will, in effect, focus on "unit" deployments rather than individual deployments.

With this basic understanding of RFFs and how they are assigned to the Air Force, we now examine how to measure their impact on the Air Force's ability to perform other missions.

---

when tracking and managing units. The Army also separately tracks the dwell time of each individual. However, these two measures are often interpreted, incorrectly, as being interchangeable.

[19] The AEF construct assumes that the Air Force is divided into five AEF pairs with approximately equal capability and that airmen will have four-month deployments over the 20-month AEF cycle (a one-to-four deployment-to-dwell ratio). The sustained operational tempo of the Air Force for the past several years had led to an increase in waiver requests for certain career fields—that is, requests that some personnel be deployed more frequently, or for longer periods, than the AEF construct suggests. The tempo-banding concept is an attempt to recognize differing demands, focus on unit type codes (UTCs) instead of individuals, and plan deployments accordingly. For example, if a combatant commander needs 232 aerial port UTCs at a given time and the Air Force has 696 of them, the Air Force would manage them with a one-to-two deployment-to-dwell ratio (i.e., there are enough UTCs so that two can be home while the third is deployed). See War and Mobilization Planning Policy Division, Headquarters U.S. Air Force (AF/A5XW), "AEF Evolution: Tempo Bands," briefing, provided to the authors on March 19, 2008.

CHAPTER THREE

Approaches for Determining the Current Impact of Joint Taskings on Personnel and Career Fields

In Chapter One, we noted that there were about 6,000 joint sourcing positions filled by Air Force personnel in 2008. This does not mean that only 6,000 personnel were affected, however. Many of these positions require deployments of 90 to 179 days, so more than one person is required in one year to fill them. For example, if all 6,000 joint sourcing positions were six-month tours, the Air Force would require 12,000 personnel to fill those positions each year.

Comparing the demand for Air Force career fields and capabilities to the availability of personnel to fill the demand allows reasonably objective assessments of the impact of joint sourcing solutions on the Air Force's combat support capability. We developed analytical tools that use available Air Force data to (1) assess the current impact of joint sourcing assignments on the Air Force, (2) forecast the future impact of filling an RFF on individual career fields, and (3) forecast the impact of filling an RFF on future AEF capabilities.

Estimating the Current Demand for Personnel

Since 2006, the Air Force Personnel Center (AFPC)/Directorate of AEF Operations (DPW) (formerly the AEF Center) at Langley AFB has had the ability to track joint sourcing assignments through updates to the Deliberate and Crisis Action Planning and Execution Segments (DCAPES) data system. We requested DCAPES data on all joint sourcing assignments from January 2006 through December 2008 that included the following information:[1]

- UTC
- Air Force Specialty Code (AFSC)
- military grade
- required arrival date in theater (year, quarter, and month)
- estimated tour length.

---

[1] These data were obtained in April 2008. We should note that while they come from an official source, we discovered late in the project that there is some dispute about the reliability of the DCAPES categorizations for ILO sourcing. When we made a separate request for updated data in July 2008, data analysts declined to break assignments down by AEF, joint sourcing, or individual augmentees due to a concern that the data were corrupt. While this was disappointing, it does not affect the prototype tool developed for this study.

Each position was identified by a unique key number that was based on the plan identification designator, the personnel increment number, and unit line number.

With these data, we can show how many personnel are supposed to arrive in theater to meet joint sourcing requirements, as illustrated in Figure 3.1.[2]

The figure contains separate lines for 365-day assignments, 179-day assignments, and joint sourcing assignments that last the "standard" (120-day) period.[3] For example, in May 2007, just under 2,500 personnel were supposed to arrive in the USCENTCOM AOR on 179-day assignments. Note that the figure does not show the number of joint sourcing positions filled by Air Force personnel each month; that number can be estimated using the arrival date and the estimated tour length (as discussed later in this chapter). Figure 3.1 provides a sense of the number of personnel moving into and out of theater to fill these assignments: Most of the personnel who arrive in May 2007 on 179-day assignments are replaced by new personnel in November 2007 (six months later). During that period new 179-day positions may have been created, and some could have been eliminated. The movement of personnel into and out of theater is most apparent in the line showing "standard" (120-day) assignments: There are clear peaks every four months starting in September 2006.

These data provide a useful representation of the impact of joint sourcing assignments on the Air Force when they are viewed cumulatively, as in Figure 3.2, which shows that—from January 2006 through December 2008—almost 40,000 Air Force personnel would have been affected by joint sourcing requirements. Again, this is a reflection of how many personnel

Figure 3.1
Joint Sourcing Demand for Air Force Personnel, by Monthly Required Delivery Date

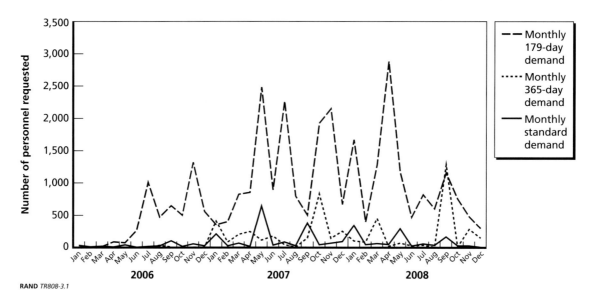

RAND TR808-3.1

---

[2] Note that although the data were collected in April 2008, they display requests through December 2008. This is because data in the system record demands that are expected to continue. For example, a 179-day position that was established in November 2007 will be filled again in May 2008 and again in November 2008. Future assignments are frequently updated and past assignments are often corrected, so these data are approximate, and requests after April 2008 could have increased.

[3] Assignments of 120 days are called "standard" because, in the 20-month AEF cycle, airmen plan to be deployed for four months (120 days) and then be at home for 16 months. There is variation in the actual tour length for the assignment categories in DCAPES. The vast majority of "standard" tours in the data set range from 120 to 125 days, but some of them are recorded as lasting 70 days or fewer. In the data set, "365-day" tours range from 221 to 455 days, but again, most are between 355 and 365 days. Ninety-three percent of the 179-day tours are between 169 and 179 days long.

Figure 3.2
Cumulative Joint Sourcing Requirement Demand for Air Force Personnel

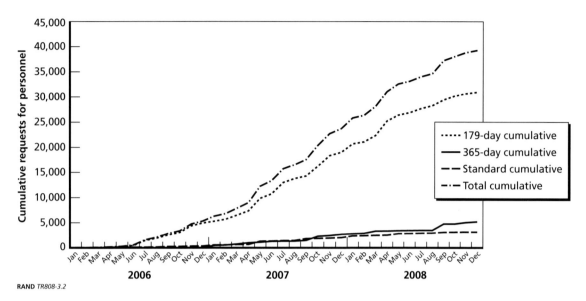

RAND *TR808-3.2*

would be moving into and out of the USCENTCOM AOR for these assignments, not an indication of how many personnel were in theater at any given time.[4] In one sense, it may be a lower bound for the number of personnel affected because, as a result of deployment limitations, Air National Guard and reserve forces use more personnel to fill some positions than the active Air Force does. For example, the guard could use four personnel, each serving for 45 days, to fill one 179-day position. Also, some people may be affected more than once by these assignments: A person who filled a 179-day tour that ended in January 2007 could volunteer to fill another one starting sometime in 2008. Nonetheless, as a representation of impact on the Air Force, displays such as this may be more informative because they show how many personnel are affected over time, rather than simply noting that there are approximately 6,000 positions being filled at any one time.

Estimating the Current Demand for Individual Career Fields

DCAPES data can also be used to better understand which Air Force career fields are currently most affected by joint sourcing demands. Table 3.1 lists (in order) the top ten enlisted and officer AFSCs requested in FY 2007. The number of requests for these personnel over the course of the year is in parentheses.

The DCAPES data indicate that there is wide variation in the level of demand for these career fields. Figure 3.3 shows the cumulative demand for the top two officer and enlisted AFSCs from Table 3.1. We see that enlisted security forces are requested far more often (over 12,000 times by December 2008) than the second-most-requested enlisted career field

---

[4]   In October 2007, there were about 25,000 airmen in the USCENTCOM AOR. At the time, there were about 526,800 personnel in the total Air Force (347,400 active-duty personnel, 105,600 guard, and 73,800 reserve). See Michael W. Wynn, Secretary of the Air Force, "Strategic Initiatives," presentation to the Armed Services Committee, U.S. House of Representatives, October 24, 2007.

Table 3.1
Most-Demanded AFSCs in FY 2007, by Number of Requests

Enlisted AFSC	Career Field	Officer AFSC	Career Field
3P0	Security forces (5,757)	32E	Civil engineer (310)
3E2	Civil engineering (pavements and construction equipment) (768)	14N	Intelligence (216)
2T1	Vehicle operations (741)	21R	Logistics readiness officer (213)
3E3	Civil engineering (structural) (651)	31P	Security forces (154)
1N0	Operations intelligence (644)	46N	Clinical nurse (122)
3E8	Civil engineering (explosive ordnance disposal) (583)	33S	Communications (102)
3E0	Civil engineering (electrical systems) (449)	16G	Air Force operations staff officer (101)
2S0	Supply management (436)	46S	Operating room nurse (91)
2T3	Vehicle and vehicle equipment maintenance (425)	41A	Health services administrator (79)
4N0	Medical (385)	42P	Clinical psychologist (69)

Figure 3.3
Cumulative Demand for the Top Two Air Force Officer and Enlisted Career Fields

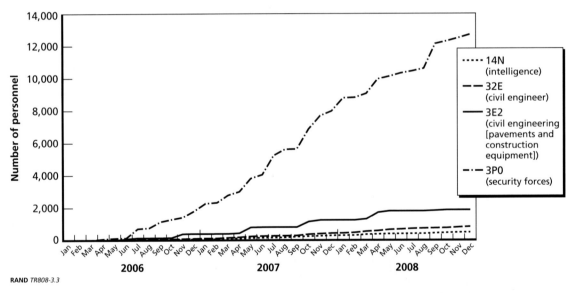

RAND *TR808-3.3*

(civil engineering [pavements and construction equipment], at just under 2,000), and both exceed the cumulative requests for the top two officer career fields.

As mentioned earlier, the AFPC/DPW data on arrival dates and expected tour lengths can be used to estimate the number of positions being filled at any given time. Figure 3.4 is an example of one such estimate for enlisted security forces on tours of various lengths between June 2007 and May 2008.[5]

---

[5] This was determined in the following way: Each position in the database has an arrival date and an expected tour length. A position was considered to exist for each month from the arrival date through the tour length. Thus, if a position has an

Figure 3.4
Estimate of Positions Filled by Air Force Enlisted Security Forces in 2007

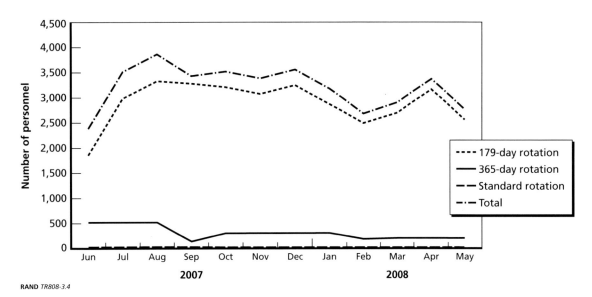

RAND *TR808-3.4*

Comparing Current Supply to Demand for Individual Career Fields

Further understanding of the impact of these assignments on the Air Force is gained by comparing the demands for joint sourcing assignments to the supply of personnel to fill them. AFPC maintains an online tool called the Interactive Demographic Analysis System (IDEAS).[6] This tool can be used to obtain population data for individual career fields broken down by various demographic characteristics, including grade. Figures 3.5 and 3.6 use this information to compare the FY 2007 cumulative demand for the top two enlisted and officer career fields (as measured by requested arrival dates in DCAPES) to the Air Force supply of active-duty personnel in these career fields. Figure 3.5 shows this comparison for enlisted security forces (3P0) and enlisted civil engineers (pavements and construction equipment, 3E2). In these figures, the horizontal axis shows the skill level or grade of personnel and the vertical axis shows demand as a percentage of the population.[7]

We see that, although enlisted security forces are in higher demand than civil engineers (as shown in Figure 3.3), the impact on the career field may, in one sense, be lower. The IDEAS

---

arrival date of January and an expected tour length of six months, it would count as one position for January through June. It is possible that this approach occasionally double-counts a position if a replacement is requested to arrive in time to allow some overlap with his or her predecessor.

[6]   Air Force Personnel Center, Interactive Demographic Analysis System (IDEAS), database.

[7]   Note that requests for enlisted joint sourcing positions are made in terms of skill level, but the IDEAS data only allow breakdowns by grade. For Figure 3.5, we have assumed that skill level 3 applies to grades up to and including airmen first class, level 5 applies to senior airmen and staff sergeants, level 7 applies to technical sergeants and master sergeants, level 9 applies to senior master sergeants, and level 0 applies to chief master sergeants. These categories accord with AFI 36-2101, "Classifying Military Personnel (Officer and Enlisted)," March 7, 2006, Table 3.8. There is some variation among career fields.

Figure 3.5
Demand Versus Active-Duty Supply for Top Two Air Force Enlisted Career Fields

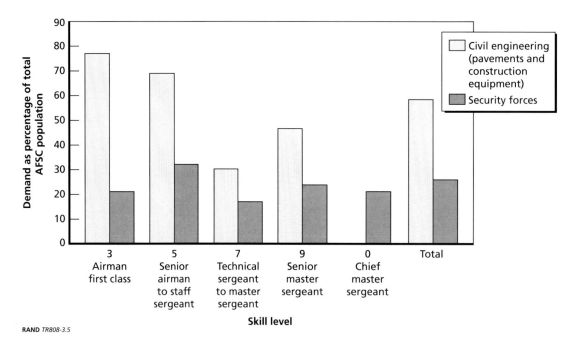

RAND *TR808-3.5*

Figure 3.6
Demand Versus Active-Duty Supply for Air Force Officer Career Fields

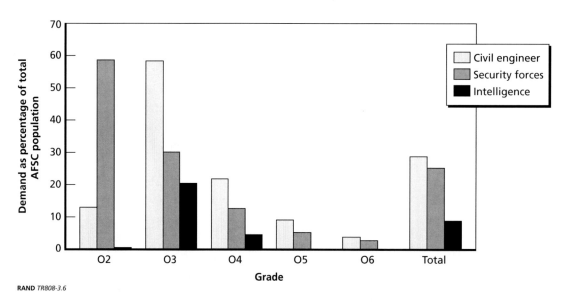

RAND *TR808-3.6*

database indicates that there are approximately 1,300 personnel in the 3E2 (civil engineering [pavements and construction equipment]) career field. Figure 3.5 shows that requests for joint sourcing assignments in this field amounted to 60 percent of the total available in the Air Force, and requests for senior airmen and staff sergeants amounted to 70 percent of the number available. Requests for enlisted security forces are comparatively lower: About

26 percent of the active-duty career field (which has approximately 25,000 enlisted personnel) and between 20 percent and 30 percent for all grades.

Figure 3.6 shows that, on the officer side, despite lower demand in terms of the number of personnel, the impact on the top two officer career fields is high.

The cumulative demand for officer civil engineers represented 30 percent of the total personnel in the career field in FY 2007 and 60 percent of the captains (grade O3). For the second-most-requested career field, intelligence, requests represented less than 10 percent of the total population. Figure 3.6 includes officer security forces in order to show the potential importance of this type of analysis: Although this career field was the fourth most demanded in FY 2007 and total requests represented only 25 percent of the career field, the demand for lieutenants represented 60 percent of the active-duty personnel available.

Note that the demands shown in Figures 3.5 and 3.6 are for joint sourcing requirements *only*. Assignments that are part of other AEF rotations are not included, nor are individual augmentee positions. In addition, these figures compare demand to the *total* active-duty population of the career field. They do not take into account that not all personnel in the career field are available for deployment, as we discuss in the next chapter.

CHAPTER FOUR

Approaches for Determining the Future Impact of Joint Taskings on Personnel, Career Fields, and AEF Capabilities

In this chapter, we continue the supply-and-demand analysis to measure the potential impact of joint sourcing assignments on individual career fields. We use available data to populate a PAF-developed analytical tool that allows the user to make detailed inputs (e.g., tour lengths, retention rates, deployment availability) related to new RFFs so that the impact of fulfilling them can be assessed. The user can display the information for the entire career field or drill down and examine deployment availability by grade or skill level (for enlisted personnel) or by rank (for officers). This is useful because it can help the Air Force better determine its capability to fulfill an RFF and present the risks of doing so. For example, the data may show that personnel with the skill or grade level specified in an RFF are already under significant strain, but personnel with the next higher (or lower) skill or grade level are available.[1]

We begin by adapting a "pyramid" of availability that has been used by some Air Force FAMs to explain why certain segments of their career fields could not be deployed in joint sourcing assignments. Figure 4.1 is an example of such a pyramid for the enlisted vehicle and vehicle equipment maintenance career field (2T3). The example is from an August 2007 quarterly career field management review. Categories of personnel who are unavailable for deployment ("nondeployable") and the numbers associated with them are listed in the left column of the pyramid; resulting decrements to the number of personnel available for deployment are shown in the band at the right.

This career field had more than 3,000 personnel assigned to it; however, several categories of personnel are unavailable for deployment. For example, 783 personnel are expected to separate, move, retire, or be otherwise unavailable for administrative or legal reasons, reducing the number available to deploy to 2,388. Other categories, including those already deployed (411 personnel) and those too junior (3-level) to be allowed to be deployed (606 personnel), ultimately reduce the number available to be deployed to 845—27 percent of the total assigned.

---

[1] The Air Force currently monitors several measures of stress on career fields. One of them is operational demand (including, among other factors, frequency of deployments and utilization of reserve forces), a second is manpower stress (which includes comparisons of requirements to funded manpower), and a third is career field health (factors such as overall staffing of the career field and retention). How well these metrics are disseminated to Air Force leadership is unclear, but personnel we interviewed who were involved in the RFF process never mentioned any of them when discussing how to measure the potential impact of fulfilling new requests for joint sourcing positions. These measures are monitored by the Directorate of Manpower, Personnel, and Services, Headquarters U.S. Air Force: Operational demand is monitored by the personnel readiness division, manpower stress is monitored by the manpower and organization division, and career field health is monitored by the force management division. Some of these measures are tracked in the Total Human Resource Management Information Service data system.

Figure 4.1
Career Field Availability Pyramid for Enlisted Vehicle and Vehicle Equipment Maintenance Career Field (2T3)

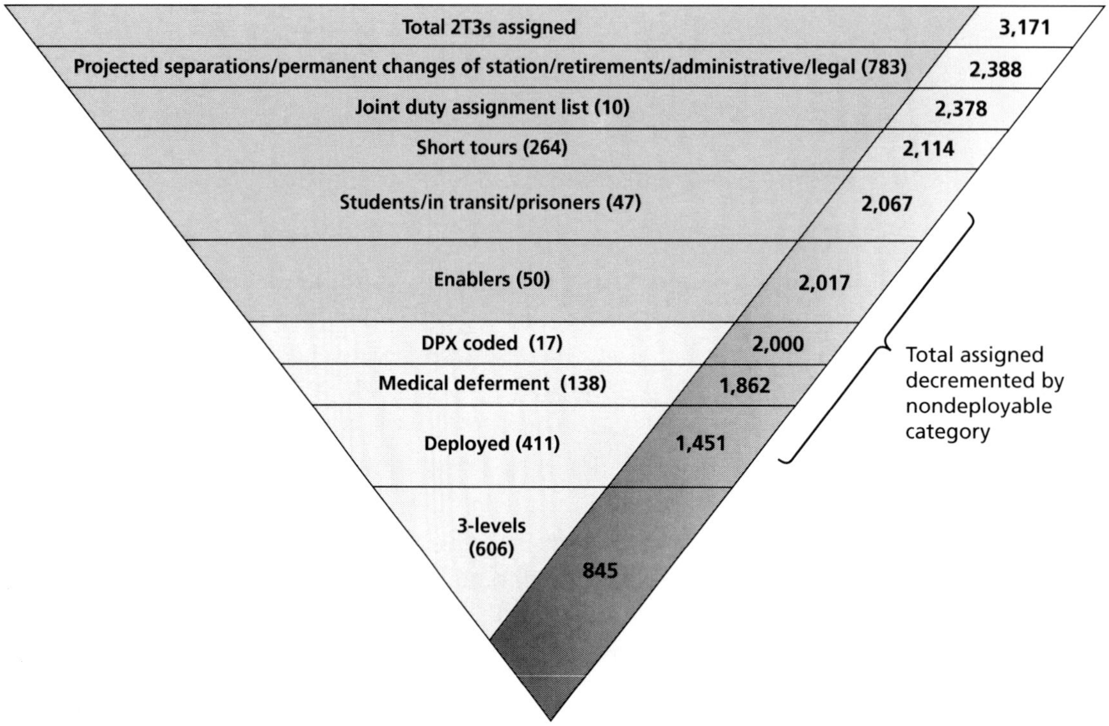

SOURCE: Installations, Logistics, and Mission Support, Headquarters U.S. Air Force, quarterly career field management review, August 2007.
RAND *TR808-4.1*

While this type of approach helps explain the categories of nondeployable personnel, one limitation of the display is that it is a "snapshot" in time that does not assist in forecasting the ability of a career field to satisfy future requests for forces. Also, although the tool shows the number of personnel currently deployed, it does not indicate the number of personnel who are undeployable because they have recently returned from a deployment. With the right tool, the Air Force could examine what happens to future deployment availability if, for example, new joint sourcing requirements were accepted, joint sourcing requirements became recurring requirements, dwell time requirements changed, or retention or accession rates changed as a result of increased demands on the career field.

With these capabilities in mind, we explored the idea of expanding the pyramid tool in a way that would allow FAMs and other managers involved in deployment planning to forecast the impact of fulfilling RFFs. The idea is displayed in Figure 4.2. Underlying Figure 4.2 is a spreadsheet that contains all of the information that was in the original pyramid: The number of personnel in the nondeployable categories is subtracted from the total number of personnel, resulting in the 845 deployable personnel. The information is displayed over time, under the assumption that some categories of information (e.g., the percentage of the career field that consists of 3-levels) vary little over time and that other categories (e.g., accessions) can be predicted based on historical trends.

Figure 4.2
Expanded Pyramid for Enlisted Vehicle and Vehicle Equipment Maintenance Career Field (2T3)

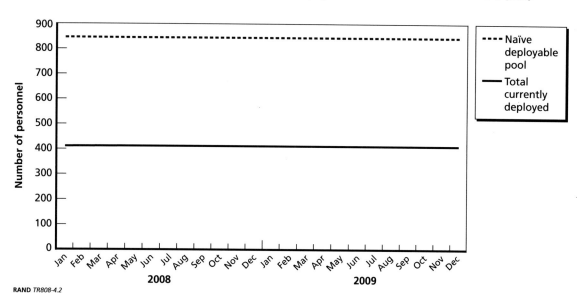

RAND *TR808-4.2*

The lower line in Figure 4.2 represents the number of 2T3 personnel deployed as of August 2007. (For the sake of developing a new tool, we have assumed that this deployment demand is initially constant from January 2008 through December 2009.) The upper line in the figure shows that there are 845 deployable personnel over this period.[2] We call this the "naïve" deployable pool because it simply subtracts the number of people in the various nondeployable categories from the total in the career field; it does not yet take into account the fact that personnel returning from deployment may not be deployable again for a certain period.

We further expand the information that can be displayed and modified, as shown in Figure 4.3, which is a screenshot of the tool's user interface. Appendix B contains more details about the data behind this display and what the user can modify, but before showing why this expansion is useful, we highlight a few sections of the display.[3]

At the top of the page, under "Current Deployments and Home Dwell Times," the user can modify how long a person can expect to stay home after a deployment before being deployed again. Note that in cell I3, the "dwell at home" for AEF (120-day) deployments, there is no entry, implying that a person who returns from deployment is immediately available to deploy again. In lines 14 and 15, the user can input details related to a new RFF. The section labeled "Non Deployable Categories" contains the information that was in the original pyramid in Figure 4.1, with the assumption that the categories are relatively unchanged over time; hence, the values remain constant in each month of 2008 and 2009. The bar chart at the lower left breaks the total number of personnel in the career field into the various nondeployable categories and the naïve deployment pool. At the lower right of the display is the graph presented in

---

[2] Projected separations, projected acquisitions, and promotions of nondeployable 3-levels to higher, deployable grades will affect the number of deployable personnel over time. For the moment, we assume that the data in the pyramid represent a steady state. We use these initial data as a jumping-off point to describe a potentially useful stream of analyses rather than as a definitive examination of a career field.

[3] A user can adjust, among other things, when retirements, separations, and permanent changes of station occur. A user can also introduce new accessions over time (something that cannot be done in a "snapshot" diagram).

Figure 4.3
Screenshot of Tool's User Interface

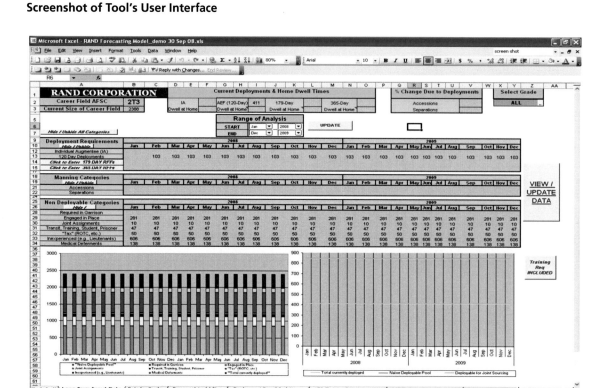

Figure 4.2, which shows the total number of deployed personnel and the naïve deployment pool. The graph in Figure 4.3 also shows a separate label for those who are deployable for joint sourcing. Because there is no entry in the "Dwell at Home" cell for AEF assignments, the naïve deployable pool and the "deployable for joint sourcing" pool are the same—anyone who has just returned from a deployment is assumed to be ready to go again—so the lines overlap.

The difference between the naïve deployment pool and the personnel available for joint sourcing appears when we take dwell time into account. Assume that personnel returning from an AEF deployment are not redeployable for four months after their return. If the user enters that information into the tool (under the "Current Deployments and Home Dwell Times" section at the top of the screen, by entering a "4" for dwell at home for AEF deployments), the graph at the lower right of Figure 4.3 changes as shown in Figure 4.4.

As in Figure 4.3, the graph still shows that 411 people are deployed, and the naïve deployable pool still shows that 845 people are deployable as of January 2009. What is new is the dashed line that shows the actual number of personnel available to deploy when dwell times at home are taken into account. The figure shows that 411 personnel are deployed and 845 personnel are in the naïve deployable pool, but only 433 personnel are available for joint sourcing assignments. Even though 845 personnel are "at home," only 433 are available to deploy

Figure 4.4
Changes in Deployment Availability When Dwell Time Is Added

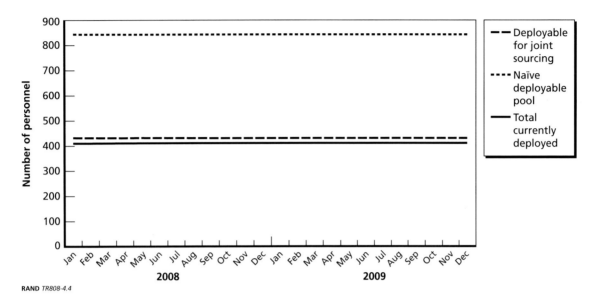

RAND *TR808-4.4*

because of the various nondeployable categories *and* the fact that personnel who have been home from a deployment for less than four months cannot be deployed again.[4]

We now consider what happens when a new RFF is received. Suppose the RFF is received in January 2008 and that it is for 70 personnel to serve in a 179-day assignment. Normally, such requests come six months in advance of the report date, so if the RFF is accepted, the deployments will start in June 2008.[5] Figure 4.5 shows the result.

Figure 4.5 shows that, starting in June 2008, the number of personnel deployed increases by 70 to 482; notice that in December 2008, the number of deployed personnel drops back to 411, since we have assumed that this joint sourcing request lasts for only six months. Also note that the naïve deployable pool decreases by 70 from June 2008 through December 2008 because of the increased number of personnel deployed. What is more important is that, in June 2008, the number of personnel deployed is greater than the number available for joint sourcing.[6] Figure 4.5 shows that, if the RFF is accepted, under current deployment and dwell time policies, the Air Force will not have enough personnel available to deploy in June 2008.[7] In order to satisfy deployment requirements at that time, either policies regarding dwell time and deployability will need to be changed or policies will need to be put into effect that could increase the size of the career field (by increasing accessions or decreasing separations). The tool accepts inputs that allow the user to explore the consequences of such policy changes. For

---

[4] The spreadsheet behind this display uses simple arithmetic to keep track of when personnel start their deployments and when they complete them. For any given month, the user entry in the "Dwell at Home" cell determines how many months recently returned personnel are counted as nondeployable.

[5] Appendix B describes how this information is entered into the tool.

[6] When the number of personnel available for joint sourcing assignments drops below the number of personnel currently deployed, the tool turns the entire line red.

[7] Note that, in this example, the dwell time for personnel on 179-day joint sourcing tours is assumed (unrealistically) to be zero. If the dwell time were increased, the shortage in personnel available to deploy would last beyond December 2008.

Figure 4.5
Result of Filling a Request for Forces

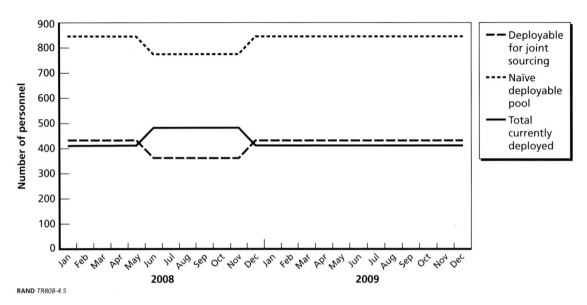

example, if the at-home dwell time for personnel returning from AEF deployments is reduced from four months to two months, the result is what is shown in Figure 4.6.[8]

The reduction in dwell time means that more personnel are available to deploy starting in June 2008. As a result, the "deployable for joint sourcing" line remains above the "total currently deployed" line, and, technically, the Air Force would have the resources to fill the new joint sourcing request.

Figure 4.6
Result of Fulfilling a Request for Forces and Modifying Dwell Time

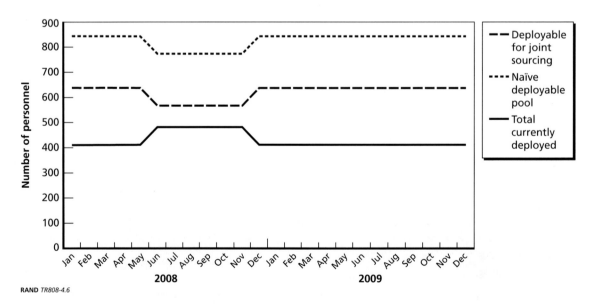

---

[8] Appendix B has more detailed examples that show how fulfilling RFFs can affect a career field.

The examples presented here make the unrealistic assumption that the size of the career field is constant over time when, in fact, it varies throughout the year because of accessions and separations; historical data can show patterns to these accessions and separations. In the next example, we begin with the same situation as that shown in Figure 4.5 (an RFF for 70 personnel who would deploy in June), but we add the assumption that every July and August, 50 people join the career field and that every October, 100 people separate. Figure 4.7 shows the result.

Figure 4.7 shows the fluctuations of the accessions and separations overlapping with the new deployments from June through December 2008. There are still too few people available to deploy under current policies, but the accessions in July and August make the shortages less extreme. Looking ahead to 2009, the figure shows the impact of the accessions-and-separations cycle without the complication of an RFF.

We continue this supply-and-demand analytical approach in the next section.

Forecasting the Impact of Joint Sourcing Assignments on AEF Capabilities

In this section, we consider two additional ways of looking at the potential impact of fulfilling joint sourcing requirements.

Assessing Steady-State Capability Shortfalls Against Future Strategic Environments

Until 2008, the analytical baseline for planning and programming in the U.S. Department of Defense (DoD) was a combination of steady-state contingencies, within what was called the "baseline security posture" (BSP), and various major combat operations. Individual contingencies in the BSP were called "vignettes" and represented steady-state scenarios in which the United States could be engaged in the future. A BSP calendar showed potential timelines for

Figure 4.7
Result of Accounting for Accessions and Separations

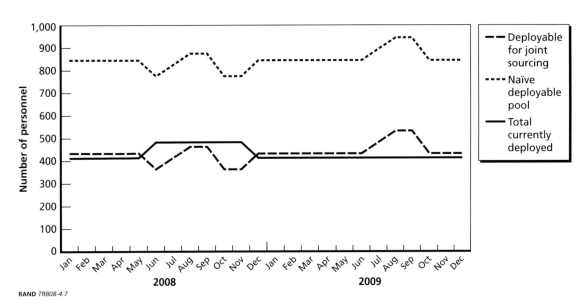

the emergence of various contingencies. Figure 4.8 is a notional representation of a seven-year portion of a BSP calendar (the official BSP calendar is not available to the general public). For example, Figure 4.8 shows that insurgency support will be needed from the middle of year 1 through almost the end of year 6, coercive campaigns will occur in years 1 and 4, and large shows of force will take place several times (and for differing lengths of time) from year 1 through year 6.[9] Since 2008, the planning environment has been called the "steady-state security posture/integrated security posture" (SSSP/ISP). The SSSP includes a set of steady-state vignettes similar to those in the BSP; the ISP includes combinations of steady-state vignettes with other contingencies.

Based on the SSSP/ISP, detailed force requirements can be developed that describe which unit types would participate in which vignettes and when. From these force requirements, it is possible, using other data sources,[10] to derive Air Force personnel requirements over time, down to the AFSC and grade level. The result represents the potential future demand for Air Force forces to meet DoD requirements.

The "supply" side of the analysis comes from several additional sources. The AEF libraries contain the planned posturing of UTCs in each AEF "bucket" (including enablers—forces that are available at all times and not assigned to an AEF). This approach provides the authorized levels of manpower in UTCs, from which it is possible to derive the Air Force's authorized steady-state capability in terms of AFSCs (again, using the MANFOR). We also use assigned levels from AFPC data and general Air Force planning factors to determine what proportion of assigned personnel, on average, would be unavailable for deployment at any time due to illness, injury, and so on. Figure 4.9 shows this supply-and-demand approach schematically.[11]

SSSP demands for personnel can be put together and compared to the Air Force's supply of personnel to assess potential shortfalls against a given future requirement (derived from a strategic environment), such as the demands represented by year 4 in Figure 4.8 (which include

Figure 4.8
Notional Sample of BSP Calendar of Vignettes

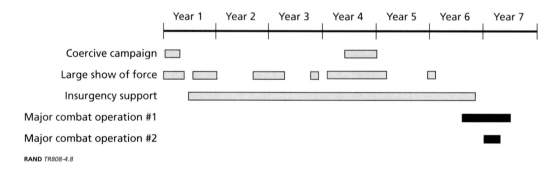

RAND *TR808-4.8*

---

[9]   Figure 4.8 is based on work by RAND colleague Patrick Mills.

[10]   Such as the Manpower Force Packaging System (MANFOR). MANFOR is a component of Manpower and Equipment Force Packaging (MEFPAK) and DCAPES. It is a database containing the UTC and title, mission capability, and manpower details for each applicable UTC. The MANFOR subsystem automates creating and maintaining manpower details for the manpower force elements associated with UTC packages. See AFI 10-401, 2006, para. 4.4.1.2.2.1. MEFPAK is the process for developing and describing standard, predefined manpower and equipment force capabilities and determining the deployment characteristics of these capabilities in support of other DoD data systems.

[11]   Figure 4.9 is derived from work by RAND colleagues Patrick Mills and David Shlapak.

Figure 4.9
Schematic of Supply-and-Demand Analysis for AEFs

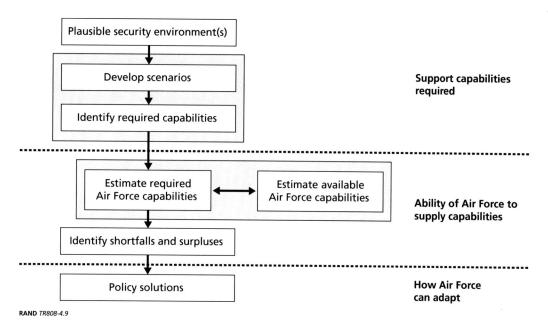

a coercive campaign, a large show of force, and insurgency support). Since the distribution of real SSSP data is restricted, Mills used notional data to produce Figure 4.10, which provides insight into the type of analysis that is possible.[12]

The figure shows the shortfalls (in terms of the number of positions) in the current AEF against these notional demands. In the bars, each color represents a career field (first three characters of an AFSC), and the height of each bar represents the number of positions that are short in the steady state. A shortfall of one position would require five positions in the normal AEF rotations to fill it, since each position in an AEF pair would be available only one-fifth of the time. The leftmost bar shows the personnel shortfall for various career fields against a notional scenario, assuming current AEF rotation policies of one-to-four dwell time (four months deployed in the AEF cycle and 16 months at home) and that enablers are always available. The next bar to the right (1:4 plus joint expeditionary tasking) adds the requirement to fill all currently requested joint expeditionary taskings ad infinitum.[13] One thing to note is that not only do joint taskings increase the shortfall, but the additional shortfall is for different career fields. Each successive pair of bars to the right shows the same metrics with a change in dwell time (1:4 to 1:3, 1:2, and 1:1, respectively). As the dwell time policy is relaxed to allow more deployed time, the shortfall is reduced substantially. Note that specifying the dwell time does not prescribe any particular deployment length. AEF policy originally specified a 90-day deployment; it is now 120 days, but this length could be varied and still meet the capabilities

---

[12] For a more detailed description of the process of assessing supply and demand using the SSSP, see Don Snyder, Patrick Mills, Manuel Carrillo, and Adam C. Resnick, *Supporting Air and Space Expeditionary Forces: Capabilities and Sustainability of Air and Space Expeditionary Forces*, Santa Monica, Calif.: RAND Corporation, MG-303-AF, 2006.

[13] We used the data on joint tasking requests from the AEF Center that showed the requested UTC and AFSC and when the request was made. From this, we derived an average level of joint taskings.

Figure 4.10
Shortfalls in Air Force Capability, by Dwell Time (using notional data)

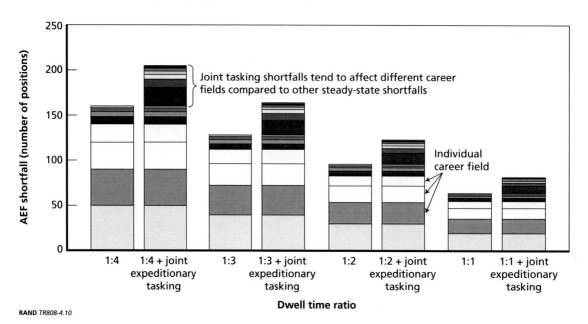

RAND TR808-4.10

specified in the figure. Indeed, the higher the deploy-to-home ratio, the more each segment would have to be lengthened to enable adequate time at home to rest and train.[14]

By using a display such as the example shown in Figure 4.10, the Air Force can anticipate the potential need to change dwell time policies or to mobilize guard and reserve forces to fill shortfalls.

Assessing Steady-State Capability Shortfalls Using UTCs

One objective of this research was to better understand the impact of joint sourcing assignments on Air Force *capabilities* related to agile combat support, and Air Force capabilities are generally presented in terms of individual UTCs. The tool presented in Figures 4.3–4.7 showed how shortfalls over time for individual career fields can be analyzed, and the tool whose outputs were presented in Figure 4.10 shows an average shortfall of individual career fields based on demands from the SSSP.[15] But some UTCs include personnel from several different career fields, and some AFSCs are assigned to several different UTCs—indeed, an installation could have an authorized position for a person in a given career field, and that position could be "postured" in more than one UTC.

FAMs and experts in AF/A5XW suggested that it would be useful to somehow combine the capabilities of the two models in order to assess changes in capability over time. One way to do this is shown schematically in Figure 4.11 using enlisted security forces as an example.

---

[14] For example, at a one-to-one ratio, the "standard" four-month AEF deployment would probably be too short: An airman would deploy for four months, be home for four months, and then redeploy for four months. A yearlong deployment would allow a year of rest at home.

[15] The results in Figure 4.10 are based on UTCs but do not take into account cross-UTC (that is, UTCs that share the same AFSCs) issues, discussed next.

Figure 4.11
Schematic for Combining AFSC and UTC Analysis

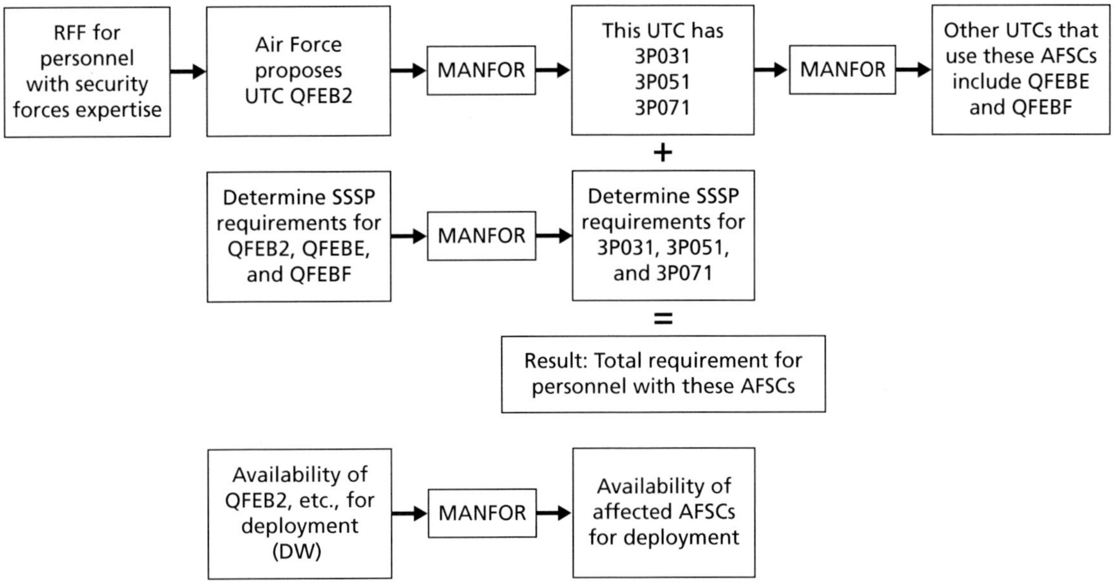

NOTE: The code "DW" indicates that the personnel are available without constraint.
RAND TR808-4.11

Suppose that an RFF for security forces is received and the Air Force considers filling it with a certain number of security force UTCs with the code QFEB2. According to MANFOR, this UTC has 13 personnel: three enlisted personnel with AFSC 3P031, nine with AFSC 3P051, and one with AFSC 3P071.[16] Again using MANFOR, we can determine all the other UTCs that make use of these three AFSCs. (There are 20 or more such UTCs described in MEFPAK, but for this example, we name only two: QFEBE and QFEBF.)

In the second row of Figure 4.11, we use the security environments described in the SSSP to determine the Air Force's demand for the three UTCs (QFEB2, QFEBE, and QFEBF). MANFOR can again be used to translate these UTC demands into the number of personnel with AFSCs 3P031, 3P051, and 3P071 whom the Air Force is expected to provide for the given security environment. Adding the proposed RFF demand to the SSSP demand provides an estimate of anticipated requirements (in terms of AFSCs) to satisfy both the forecast SSSP demands and current contingency demands.

On the supply side, the AEF library can be used to determine how the affected UTCs (QFEB2, QFEBE, and so forth) are "postured"—for example, a code of "DW" means that they are available without constraint. This availability, or supply, can be compared to the anticipated demand. Figure 4.12 uses notional data to show such a comparison.

We again assume that a request for security forces has been received and that the Air Force proposes to satisfy it using personnel in UTC QFEB2. The "SSSP demand" line in Figure 4.12 shows the determination of the demand for security force personnel based on *all* UTCs that are affected by the AFSCs in QFEB2 (we have used the yearlong period from June 2007 to May 2008 to make use of current data on deployments to OIF and OEF). The "AEF library capability" line shows the planned supply of personnel with AFSCs 3P031, 3P051,

---

[16] This information is from a MANFOR database.

Figure 4.12
Capability Supply-and-Demand Comparison Example for Security Forces

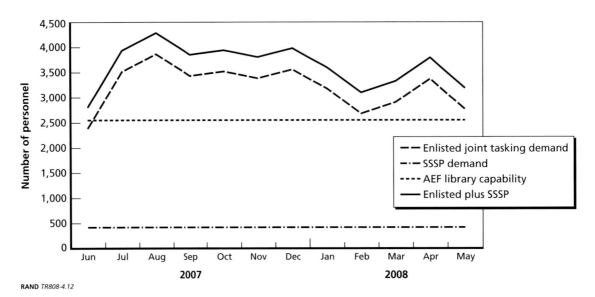

RAND *TR808-4.12*

and 3P071, based on the posturing of all UTCs that include those personnel.[17] We see that the Air Force is comfortably postured to satisfy SSSP demands, with 2,500 personnel planned to be available to meet a demand for fewer than 500.[18]

However, the OIF/OEF demands for security personnel (the enlisted joint tasking demand, as expressed in the AFPC/DPW data discussed in Chapter Two) exceed the AEF library supply, and adding the two demands together (the "Enlisted plus SSSP" line) causes the shortfall to look worse.[19]

Figures 4.5, 4.10, and 4.12 tell slightly different stories, all of which are important in different contexts. Figure 4.5 allows a FAM to determine the potential impact of a new RFF on his or her AFSC's ability to meet currently known deployment requirements. The analysis shown in Figure 4.10 allows a decisionmaker to assess the potential impact of RFFs for individual capabilities (UTCs) on future AEF capabilities. Figure 4.12 shows the potential shortages over time of individual AFSCs that result from forecast demands placed on them by *all* UTCs required by the SSSP and joint sourcing requirements.

In fact, in the case of security forces, the impact of this high demand has already been recognized and dealt with: first by "reaching forward" in the AEF cycle to deploy personnel before they were originally scheduled and second by increasing the number of personnel who are deployed for six-month assignments instead of four-month assignments and changing to a one-to-one deploy-to-dwell posture. The tool described in this section was not used to predict

---

[17] Note that this supply is based on the standard AEF deployment of 90 days, which, as we know, is no longer applicable to security forces.

[18] This analysis is based on only one security environment. It might be useful to compare the results using other security environments. Also, UTC posturing may overstate availability—because personnel may be postured in multiple UTCs. The AEF UTC Reporting Tool is supposed to take this into account.

[19] Note that the demand shown in Figure 4.11 is only for SSSP and joint sourcing demands. Other security force taskings, such as individual augmentee assignments, are not included.

or anticipate the need for these changes, but it could be useful for planning with other career fields and UTCs.

A display such as that in Figure 4.12 makes it immediately clear to a FAM or AEF planner that a new RFF demand cannot be satisfied—indeed, that something must be done to the supply to meet current demand.

Summary

This chapter highlighted the Air Force's analytical resources for identifying the impact of joint sourcing solutions on personnel, career fields, and capabilities. First, data available from AFPC/DPW and IDEAS enables detailed analysis of the current stresses on personnel and individual career fields by grade and skill level. Second, data are available to populate a tool (such as that described in Figures 4.3–4.7) to help FAMs better inform Air Force leadership of the potential risks to individual career fields of filling future RFFs, taking into account changing tour lengths, changes in retention rates, and changes in deployment availability. Finally, data are currently available to enable an examination of the impact of joint taskings on AEF *capabilities* (as described in Figures 4.10 and 4.12).

CHAPTER FIVE

Other Potential Impacts of Joint Taskings

Comparing the forecast demand for Air Force capabilities to the forecast availability of personnel to fill the demand allows an objective assessment of the impact of joint taskings on the Air Force's combat capability by highlighting the size and timing of potential personnel shortages. Other ways that joint taskings affect personnel and missions are more difficult to measure. In this chapter, we discuss several factors related to the impact of joint sourcing assignments that were mentioned in our interviews by individuals who have served in these assignments, continental U.S. commanders who have to deal with the consequences of absent personnel, and various staffers who participate in the RFF process. These comments arose in discussions related to data availability; they are not the result of surveying a random sample of personnel or of conducting structured interviews to collect assessments on specific topics.

The In-Garrison Impact of Joint Sourcing Assignments

In our research, we attempted to address the question of how joint taskings affect in-garrison operations. We were unable to do this for several reasons. First, standard metrics for unit performance do not exist and, for a variety of reasons, would be very difficult to develop, so it is difficult to understand how the loss of individuals affects unit performance. The loss of one officer to a joint sourcing assignment would clearly affect a headquarters unit that is already understaffed; it would also affect a training unit that needs instructors, but it would be difficult to compare the impact on the two units. Second, filling joint sourcing assignments can affect unit services that are not directly related to mission accomplishment. For example, if joint sourcing assignments resulted in a shortage of security personnel at a base, one response could be to close (or limit the hours of) some entrances to the base. This could represent an inconvenience for military and civilian personnel, but mission impact would be difficult to measure. Third, it is impossible to distinguish the effects of joint sourcing missions from those of other Air Force deployments, as we discuss further in this chapter. Finally, Air Force personnel (and personnel in other services) tend to have a "can-do" attitude, which means that they will work very hard to accomplish their mission. Assessing the breaking point for most activities presents a significant challenge. Thus, it may not be obvious that a unit is overstressed until the loss of one more person to a deployment leads to some sort of mission failure.

Our discussions provided insight into challenges related to uncovering how deployments affect home-station operations.

As we have seen, airmen deploy for several different types of missions: as part of an AEF ("blue on blue"), as individual augmentees, and as personnel filling joint taskings. All of these categories currently support OIF, OEF, and other contingency operations. There is no way to differentiate the impact of different types of deployment, but we can seek to understand the impact of deployments in general.

One difference between joint tasking assignments and blue-on-blue deployments, though, is that joint taskings represent unpredictable reductions in personnel at home stations. Unlike AEF deployments, which have some measure of predictability, new RFFs can come at any time. As we have discussed, certain career fields, such as security forces, tend to be particularly hard hit, and some (again, such as security forces) have significant in-garrison roles.

The Army and the Air Force have different perspectives on home-station capability, and understanding one provides insight into the other. Army units are seen and treated as cohesive wholes. Their in-garrison role is to train and prepare for deployments abroad. When units are deployed, Army civilians and contractors who are left behind maintain and provide security for a post with a significantly lower population than before the deployment.[1]

Air Force deployments usually take place in the AEF construct, and since an AEF is made up of a combination of assets located at different bases (perhaps including fighter, bomber, and mobility bases), some elements (or personnel) of a given unit may deploy while others remain at their home base. For example, a fighter base may send some aircraft, pilots, and maintenance personnel forward. Unlike the Army, however, those who are deployed may be responsible for activities at the base that will be left undone while they are away.

In addition, in the Air Force, virtually everyone is eligible to deploy, so units have two ongoing missions: to maintain the force during wartime and to continually rejuvenate the force. The functional distinctions of the bases may allow many efficiencies, but this also means that the base must stay open and the home mission—of preparing for war and of supporting the war—must continue. At the same time, the full range of base support functions must remain available. An operating base cannot afford to lose, for example, all of its security personnel, and it would not be the case that all of them would deploy at the same time as part of the AEF cycle.

This structure means that bases can be hard hit by deployments (both AEF and joint sourcing) and must continue operating with reduced personnel. That is, in fact, what happens. In the absence of their colleagues, airmen work longer hours. (We spoke to one individual whose hours were so long that his young child thought he was on deployment.) Services may have reduced hours, and the base may "accept some risk" in some areas (e.g., it might have fewer security patrols on the flightline).

Joint taskings use ready forces but may degrade the unit's ability to rejuvenate the force (especially if the deployments are unanticipated). There are fewer personnel to provide training to new troops. Some workload may not receive sufficient attention, or some jobs may not be accomplished, and local exercises or contingency operations may be affected. Taskings may cause staff remaining behind to work long hours, leading to reduced productivity. However, all of these home-station risks are taken in support of the mission overseas.

---

[1] The U.S. Army's Installation Management Command "oversees all facets of installation management such as construction; barracks and family housing; family care; food management; environmental programs; well-being; Soldier and Family morale, welfare and recreation programs; logistics; public works and installation funding" (U.S. Army Installation Management Command, "History," web page, undated). The vast majority of Army post functions are performed by civilians, according to a January 27, 2009, conversation with a program manager in the Office of the Assistant Chief of Staff for Installation Management, Plans Division.

There is no metric for measuring levels of in-garrison capability, or even a binary measure of whether a base is broken. Instead, Air Force bases must make do with reduced staffing levels by working harder and accepting risk. The personnel with whom we spoke agreed that these were necessary (if not easy) sacrifices during wartime. Commanders back home do not necessarily distinguish the source of the pain. They just know they have to manage with whatever level of resources they have. The key is managing risks.

The Impact of Joint Sourcing Assignments on Training, Careers, and Retention

As part of our research, we interviewed 12 airmen who had recently served on joint taskings. This was not in any sense a representative sample of individuals serving in these assignments; they were a convenience sampling group that resulted from the suggestion of one person we interviewed about process that we should talk to a colleague who had served on such an assignment. Eleven of the 12 personnel we interviewed were officers, ten were logistics readiness officers, ten were deployed to Afghanistan, and two had recently returned from Iraq; nine had served 365-day tours, and three were on 179-day tours. Next, we briefly discuss several of the topics raised in these interviews—some of which warrant further research to better understand their importance.

Selection Processes of 179-Day and 365-Day Tours

One point highlighted by those we interviewed was the difference in the selection process of personnel for 179-day tours and 365-day tours. The shorter tours are managed within the AEF process and are, in the following sense, less disruptive: An RFF for a 179-day tour generally goes to someone who is in the deployment/on-call phase of the AEF cycle. The longer tours are managed on an individual basis by AFPC. Personnel can volunteer for these assignments, but the eligibility of nonvolunteers is based on their "short-tour return date" (i.e., how long it has been since they returned from a deployment that lasted more than 180 days).[2] Personnel who have recently returned from a short tour are least eligible to be involuntarily deployed; those who have never served a short tour are most eligible to be deployed. Several personnel we interviewed said that, technically, they were volunteers for their 365-day tours, but the reason they volunteered was that they were advised by AFPC that they were at the top of the non-volunteer eligibility list because of their short-tour return date. Our interviewees indicated that volunteers were given more input into selecting their follow-on assignments. Given that they would probably be selected anyway, they "volunteered." (They were careful to point out this distinction.)[3]

---

[2] AFI 36-2110, "Personnel: Assignments," April 20, 2005, p. 256, provides the formal definition of a short tour. For example, an individual receives credit for an overseas "short" tour if the assignment would last 24 months accompanied (the service member takes his or her family) or less than 18 months unaccompanied.

[3] In September 2008, the Air Force made some changes to how 365-day tours are assigned. The net result, according to a September 19, 2008, AFPC release, will be to give airmen destined to serve those yearlong deployments more advance notice than they currently get. The service has nearly 2,000 airmen in 365-day deployments, and about one-third of those received less than 60 days' notice. "'These changes are designed to streamline the process and provide airmen adequate time to prepare themselves and their families before departing,' said Maj. Gen. K. C. McClain, AFPC commander" (Kat Bailey,

Predeployment Experiences

Training for Air Force personnel selected for joint tasking assignments is managed by the 2nd Air Force through the 602d Training Group (Provisional) and subordinate detachments at Army training locations.[4]

Those we interviewed had predeployment training that lasted from two to three months and generally emphasized combat skills training. All of the personnel we interviewed said that the training was too long; however, we do not know if this complaint is typical.

Criticisms of the training itself were that it was not necessary (e.g., the personnel did not need combat skills training if they were not going to go "outside the wire" during their assignment) and that it was not appropriate. For example, some personnel who knew they were going to Afghanistan were trained in procedures that were applicable only to Iraq.

A more important criticism related to training is that, for active-duty Air Force personnel, training time does not count toward deployment time. Thus, when training is taken into account, personnel who were deployed on a 179-day joint tasking could easily be away from home for eight months, and those on 365-day tours could be gone for 14 or 15 months, but they would be credited for being deployed for the shorter period. For Air National Guard and reserve-component personnel, some training time can be included in total deployment time.[5] Similarly, Army personnel train as a unit at their home bases, so they also do not accumulate "deployment credit" for predeployment training activities that keep them away from home for extended periods.

Deployment Experiences

Individual experiences are, by their very nature, subjective and unique. Different individuals in the same circumstances may have entirely different experiences. We certainly found this to be the case. Some personnel viewed their joint taskings deployment experiences very positively: One individual who had been sent on a 179-day deployment that ended up lasting longer than ten months reported trying to stay for a full year. These individuals tended to have had positive and respectful interactions with members of other services. A couple of our interviewees had

---

"Policy Changes Benefit Airmen Headed for 365-Day Deployments," Randolph Air Force Base, Tex.: Air Force Personnel Center Public Affairs, September 19, 2008).

[4] The detachments "interface with Army representatives, relieve the troop commander of administrative burden, provide force accounting, and resolve issues impacting the ability to organize, train, and equip ILO Airmen." There are about 20 training locations for Army combat skills training, specialty training (such as postal services or communications), or Air Force blue-on-blue training (2nd Air Force, "In-Lieu-Of Training," briefing, provided to the authors in October 2007a; 2nd Air Force, "In-Lieu-Of Training Concept of Operations (CONOPS)," draft, undated, provided to the authors in October 2007b.

[5] In January 2007, the SecDef directed that mobilization of reserve-component ground forces be managed on a unit basis and that involuntary mobilizations of reserve-component units and members be limited to a maximum of one year. See Robert M. Gates, "Utilization of the Total Force," memorandum, January 19, 2007.

Prior to this policy, the Army mobilized troops for 16–18 months to allow four months of unit training and 12 months of deployed time. With the new policy, some portion of the four months of training must be conducted in the year prior to mobilization, but this is not easy. In September 2007, the Army was developing an approach that would move about three-quarters of the required training formally done after mobilization to the year before mobilization. The goal was to limit postmobilization training to just 45 days, allowing for 320 days of deployment—still less than a full year of "boots on the ground." See Defense Science Board Task Force, *Deployment of Members of the National Guard and Reserve in the Global War on Terrorism*, Washington, D.C.: Office of the Under Secretary of Defense for Acquisition, Technology, and Logistics, September 2007, p. 21.

very negative experiences, to the point that they indicated they would consider leaving the Air Force if tapped for a similar tour of duty. This was not a representative sample, so it is impossible to draw out general implications, but in both cases, it appeared that a clash in service cultures led to difficulties, and this might be a fruitful area of future research.

One issue that frequently arose in our small interview sample was the disconnect between what personnel had been trained to do in their Air Force positions and what they were asked to do when deployed on joint taskings. A comparison of logistics officer specialties in Table 5.1 demonstrates that, for example, the subspecialties in the Army logistics officer MOS are much broader than in the Air Force logistics readiness officer AFSC. For example, in the Army, that MOS includes the quartermaster role (MOS 92A),[6] so if a quartermaster position needs to be filled, it would be logical for an RFF to be for a logistics readiness officer. However, while the Air Force logistics readiness officer field includes broad responsibilities, it is not the case that any Air Force logistics readiness officer would be appropriate to perform quartermaster duties.

Several of the interviewees arrived in theater without knowing what their eventual jobs would be and had to wait a couple of days or weeks to find out. This was a source of frustration whenever it occurred. One person we interviewed found that the original job he had been expected to fill no longer existed when he arrived.

Some of the individuals appreciated the opportunity to work with other services, but others had mixed experiences. One joked that those who had served on joint taskings referred to the experience as an "Air Force appreciation tour."

Postdeployment Experiences

We speculated that individuals who were away from their continental U.S. Air Force jobs for a year might need refresher training upon their return—especially if the job they performed in their joint tasking was significantly different from their normal job in the Air Force. For the most part, those we interviewed said this was not the case. One person noted that while he was deployed, the Air Force introduced a new automated system to write orders and that officer performance reports, enlisted performance reports, and awards had been automated; he said he returned to a "new Air Force," but he did not indicate that any type of transition training would have been useful. Instead, he felt that he was able to learn the new system about as quickly and with the same level of ease as he would have had he not been deployed, so it was merely a question of timing.

The Impact of a Joint Sourcing Deployment on an Individual's Career

An issue that frequently arose was the question of how airmen are administratively treated during longer deployments. Our interviewees distinguished among administrative control, tactical control, and operational control. Officers on 365-day deployments expressed concern that administrative control passed from the Air Force to their supported service. They indicated that each service had particular code words that tended to be used as signals of different types of performance in their officer performance reports and that, as a result, an Army rater might not use the language necessary to ensure the promotion of an Air Force officer or airman. We did not hear any evidence that this actually happened, but the source of the officer

---

[6] "The Quartermaster Officer provides supply support for soldiers and units in field services, aerial delivery and material and distribution management" (U.S. Army, "Quartermaster Officer (92)," web page, undated).

Table 5.1
Comparison of Logistics Officer Specialties

Air Force	Army	Marine Corps	Navy
Aviation, ship, and submarine maintenance			
21A Aircraft maintenance	15D Aviation logistics	6002 Aircraft maintenance	144X Restricted line (engineering duty officer)
		5902 Limited-duty officer (aviation elect maintenance)	152X Restricted line (aviation maintenance)
			613X Limited-duty officer (engineering/repair—surface)
			623X Limited-duty officer (engineering/repair—submarine)
			633X Limited-duty officer (aviation maintenance)
Ordnance, munition, and missile maintenance			
21M Munitions and missile maintenance subspecialty	89E Explosive ordnance disposal	Only warrant officers	616X Limited-duty officer (ordnance—surface)
21MxC Nuclear	91A Maintenance and munitions	Only warrant officers	626X Limited-duty officer (ordnance—submarine)
			636X Limited-duty officer (ordnance—aviation)
			648X Limited-duty officer (explosive ordnance disposal)
Readiness, transportation, and supply			
21R Logistics readiness	90A Logistics	0402 Logistics	310X Staff corps (supply corps)
	88A Transportation—general	3002 Ground supply	6510 Limited-duty officer (supply corps)
	88B Traffic management	3502 Motor transport	Subspecialties
	88C Marine and terminal operations	6602 Aviation supply	1301 Supply acquisition—distribution
	88D Motor/rail		1302 Systems inventory management
	92A Quartermaster—general		1304 Transportation logistics management
	92D Aerial delivery and material		1305 Retailing
	92F Petroleum and water		1306 Acquisition and contract management
			1307 Petroleum management

NOTE: Table does not include warrant officer specialties. In addition, there are no subspecialties unless shown. See Raymond E. Conley and Albert A. Robbert, *Air Force Officer Specialty Structure: Reviewing the Fundamentals*, Santa Monica, Calif.: RAND Corporation, TR-637-AF, 2009, p. 28, Table 4.2.

performance report may be something for the Air Force to consider when evaluating personnel for promotion after they have deployed on joint taskings.

We heard that one general officer had spread the message that anyone seeking eventual promotion to the most senior levels would need to have deployed, so serving in a joint tasking position would fill that requirement for those who had otherwise missed being deployed. One individual specifically referred to the need to be deployed for promotion as one of the benefits of deployment and recommended it to other officers who had not yet deployed.

The Impact of Joint Sourcing Deployments on Different Career Fields

Certain career implications vary by length of joint tasking assignment. There is a significant difference between how 365-day tours and shorter deployments are treated. Long deployments fall into the "permanent change of station" category, are managed by the AFPC at Randolph AFB, and are not part of the AEF cycle. Such deployments to date have come with the so-called "seven-day option." This means that eligible airmen can choose to retire or separate rather than accept a 365-day deployment.

This option can have serious implications for individual career fields with a significant demand for 365-day deployments. We heard of cases in which several people chose to retire rather than deploy when faced with a need to fill a particular RFF. This meant that filling a single RFF led both to the Air Force's permanent loss of several personnel who retired or separated and to a unit's loss of capability for Air Force requirements that were fulfilled by the airmen who ultimately accepted the deployment. This has increased the strain of joint taskings on some career fields, such as logistics readiness officers.

Since members of stressed career fields usually have frequent deployments, the choice to take the seven-day option is not surprising. Even the most willing airmen may have developing family circumstances that make deployment extremely problematic, for example. One or two of our interviewees indicated that their 365-day deployments in joint tasking positions working with other services and basically separated from the Air Force (and its culture, processes, support network, and so on) were so difficult that they would retire—or even separate—rather than serve again in the same conditions.

Conclusion

The potential impact of joint sourcing assignments in the various areas discussed in this chapter is difficult to measure; however, it is important to note that these concerns have been raised by commanders and personnel who have served in joint sourcing assignments. In particular, the impact of these assignments on retention and on individual career development deserves further study.

CHAPTER SIX

Conclusions and Recommendations

The environments of OIF and OEF have required all the military services to respond in new ways to emerging requirements for new types of missions. Since its inception in 2004, the GFM process has functioned reasonably well in ensuring that new tasks can, if necessary, be accomplished by personnel provided by a service other than the "preferred" provider. In the course of satisfying these needs, all the services need to understand the potential impact of emerging requirements on individuals, units, and combat capabilities. For the Air Force, which attempts to maintain constant readiness for all of its units, this understanding is particularly important to making resource allocation decisions that will ensure that it can satisfy the full range of demands for its capabilities.

Chapter Three described a relatively simple tool that can be used to forecast the impact of filling emergent requirements on individual career fields and UTCs.[1] In extensive discussions with FAMs, AEF planners (from AF/A5X), managers involved with personnel readiness (Personnel Readiness Division, Headquarters U.S. Air Force [AF/A1PR]), and senior executives, we found great interest in the tool's capabilities. FAMs felt that it could be used to more effectively communicate with senior leaders but expressed concern that maintaining such a tool would merely add another administrative burden to them. They also noted the importance of ensuring that all career fields that might use the tool have access to the same data sources. Our AF/A1PR contacts indicated that the standardized data sources needed to populate the spreadsheets for the tool are available and that doing so would not be difficult or time-consuming. AF/A1PR is in the process of setting up a new office that will standardize training for FAMs; our first recommendation is that the new office pursue development of the personnel forecasting model to ensure that data sources are standardized, most data cells in the model are filled automatically from the standardized sources, FAMs have easy access to the tool, and FAMs have the flexibility to make inputs that are unique to their career fields. The tool is a relatively simple forecasting model that could be developed by a number of business software contractors. We recommend that the Air Force pursue the development and utilization of such a tool.

Determining the potential impact of joint taskings on Air Force combat capabilities is more complicated, and, as discussed here, requires the use of a more sophisticated (and, generally, classified) tool that translates forecast capability demands based on the SSSP into Air Force UTC and career field requirements. We recommend that the Air Force adopt such a forecasting model and work to continue to refine this capability.

---

[1] At least three offices in Air Force headquarters develop a variety of measures for operational demand, manpower stress, and career field health, but the tools discussed in Chapters Three and Four could provide another option to clearly show the impact, by various demographics (grade, AFSC, skill level), of joint taskings in a way that goes beyond stating the number of positions that Air Force personnel are filling.

Standardized metrics for garrison-level impact of joint taskings do not currently exist, and our discussions with a variety of unit, command, and headquarters personnel lead us to believe that the diverse nature of missions of Air Force units would make standard measures difficult to develop. The career field and combat capability tools discussed in this report may be the best substitute; nonetheless, the Air Force should continue to monitor feedback from personnel who have participated in joint sourcing assignments—both explicit, in the form of after-action reports, and implicit, in the form of continuation rates—to ensure that personal, family, career, and career field stresses are understood and addressed.

APPENDIX A

Details of the Joint Sourcing Process

Chapter Two briefly described the joint sourcing process, with Figure 2.1 showing the major organizations involved. This appendix provides more details about how rotational and emergent force requirements are established and also describes how the Air Force responds to RFFs.

Determination of Requirements for Rotational Forces Is Calendar-Driven

The Joint Staff produces the Rotational Force Allocation Plan, which gives strategic-level planning guidance for rotational forces to the primary joint force provider, COCOMs, and services.[1] Requirements for rotational forces, including for exercises, contingencies, and individual augmentees,[2] are determined on an annual basis and published in the GFM Allocation Plan. The plan provides a summary of all SecDef-approved force allocation actions.[3]

A notional timeline for the rotational allocation process from December 2007 is shown in Figure A.1. In the first quarter (October–December) of the annual cycle,[4] the GFM Board reviews and prioritizes COCOM requirements for the next two years. After this approval, the primary force provider develops a draft rotational force allocation plan. In the second quarter, the GFM Board meets to review and approve the draft rotational plan and forwards it to the SecDef for approval. In the third quarter, the board reviews the plan for any changes that may have been identified since SecDef approval, and in the fourth quarter, the board begins preparing for the next cycle by asking COCOMs for new requirements. If necessary, decisions of the board are reviewed by a CJCS "tank" session (which includes the chiefs of all the services or their representatives).

---

[1] Ferriter and Burdon, 2007.

[2] IAs are "unfunded temporary duty positions (military or civilian) requested to augment a supported combatant commander's or governmental agency's staff operations during contingencies. Similar to requests for forces (RFFs) in support of contingencies, [individual augmentee] requirements are inherently temporary in nature and are not to be used to solve permanent manning or capability shortages" (AFI 10-401, 2006, para. 9.4.3).

[3] AF/A5XJ, 2007.

[4] Again, this timeline is subject to change. This description is from Ferriter and Burdon, 2007, and loosely follows Figure A.1.

43

Figure A.1
Notional Global Force Management Timeline

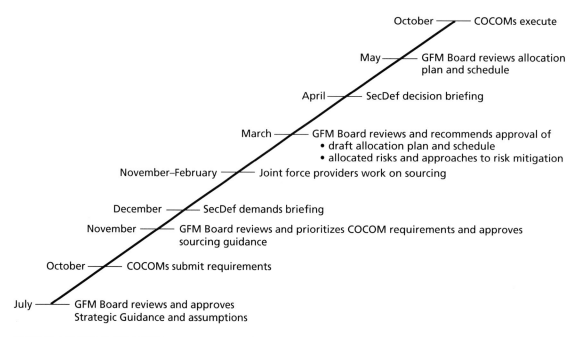

SOURCE: JCS J3/JOD-GFM, 2007.
NOTE: The timeline for the process has been revised several times, most recently in June 2008.
RAND *TR808-A.1*

Emergent Forces Requirements Are Need-Driven

When emergent force requirements cannot be satisfied using existing forces available to COCOMs, the COCOMs submit an RFF. The RFF process involves the same organizations as requests for rotational forces but with a different time frame and additional guidance and procedures. In this section, we discuss how RFFs originate and are validated as well as how the Air Force makes inputs into the process that identifies and executes a joint sourcing solution.

How a Request for Forces Originates and Is Validated

When a unit in theater develops, or is assigned, a new requirement, the field commander submits a unit request for forces (URF) to the COCOM staff, which determines whether the request can be filled with existing resources.[5] If they determine that there are not sufficient resources in the AOR, the COCOM staff, working in concert with its component service staffs (U.S. Central Command Air Forces, U.S. Navy Central Command, ARCENT) develops an RFF, which is made up of multiple URFs.[6]

The Joint Staff regional Joint Operations Directorate (JOD) reviews the draft RFF and generates requests for information that the COCOM will answer in order to clarify the nature

---

[5]   New missions can come from the brigade level, but the endorsements always come from the general officer level, according to a December 26, 2007, interview with Joint Action Coordinating Office (JACO) personnel.

[6]   Discussions with A3O personnel, October 29, 2007. In December 2007, about two-thirds of the RFFs were validated at the COCOM level.

of the request. The COCOM then formally "releases" the draft RFF to the Joint Staff and it is entered into a software system called the Joint Event Scheduling System (JESS).[7] For requests from USCENTCOM, USCENTCOM J3 (the operations directorate) enters the RFF in the Force Requirements Enhanced Database (FRED), which assigns it a force tracking number.[8] The FRED entry includes a note about whether alternative sourcing solutions through joint sourcing are acceptable. For example, an initial request might be for transport and specifically mention C-130s, but FRED will note that other options will be considered to meet the capability.[9] The left side of Figure A.2 summarizes these steps, and the right side identifies the steps taken to validate the RFF, as described next.

Once released by the COCOM, the RFF goes forward to J3/JOD-GFM for vetting and validation. Validation can take three days, during which time the JOD can submit more requests for information. As of December 2007, about 90 percent of the RFFs submitted were validated.[10]

When the regional JOD accepts the RFF for staffing, a target date is selected for inclusion of the RFF in the SecDef Operations Book (SDOB, the document used to present the request to the SecDef), which determines the timing for other required staff actions. Next, an action officer puts together a Joint Staff Action Package, which includes the RFF, a coordination form (the Joint Staff Form 136), a draft execution order, and a transmittal memorandum. At the same time, the action officer staffs the RFF to the appropriate joint force provider, usually USJFCOM, allowing about 21 days for a response.[11] Finally, the RFF is entered into the "logbook tasker," a spreadsheet that is available online to action officers involved in the process. A copy is also sent to Air Force headquarters and supporting COCOMs.[12] As noted in Figure A.2, in FY 2008, about one in three RFFs was stopped at the USCENTCOM level. Almost 90 percent of RFFs that made it to the Joint Staff were validated.

How a Joint Sourcing Solution Is Identified

Validated RFFs are sent to the joint force provider. For conventional forces (which, in the case of OIF and OEF, is almost always the case) this is USJFCOM. The logbook tasker is also used to forward the RFF and any additional guidance about the nature of the request to the service component force providers. USJFCOM also forwards the RFF to service providers in other COCOMs (e.g., U.S. European Command, U.S. Pacific Command).[13] For the Air Force, the

---

[7] Use of JESS was initiated in November 2008. Before that time, RFFs were entered into the Joint Force Requirements Management system. The Joint Staff issued guidelines for how the RFFs should be written.

[8] Discussion with Global Combat Support, Headquarters U.S. Air Force (AF/A4/7Z), personnel, November 30, 2007.

[9] JCS J3/JOD-GFM, 2007.

[10] JCS J3/JOD-GFM, 2007.

[11] The Joint Staff targets a specific joint force provider, depending on the nature of the RFF. USJFCOM must run sourcing recommendations through the joint force providers.

[12] AFI 10-401, 2006, para. 1.10.4.1.

[13] According to interviews with the J3/JOD-GFM and AF/A4/A7Z personnel, service force providers are supposed to check with their service components in other COCOMs. However, the reality is that USJFCOM asks the force providers and the service components simultaneously and, in some cases, forces are double-counted as a result.

Figure A.2
Process from URF to RFF Validation

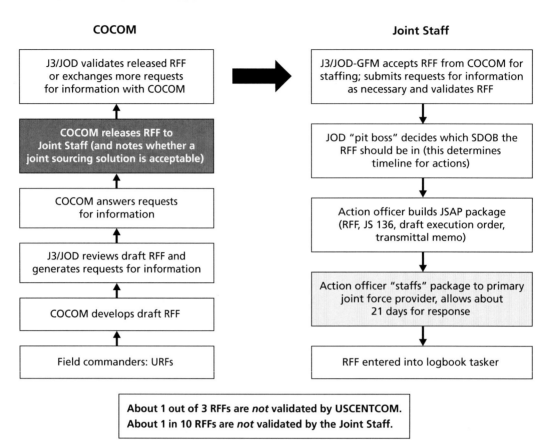

About 1 out of 3 RFFs are *not* validated by USCENTCOM.
About 1 in 10 RFFs are *not* validated by the Joint Staff.

SOURCE: Adapted from JCS J3/JOD-GFM, 2007.
RAND *TR808-A.2*

RFF is simultaneously sent to the Air Force Operations Group, Current Operations (A3O-AOB).[14] The other services have a similar process.[15]

USJFCOM coordinates with supporting COCOMs and services to decide which force provider should fill the RFF; Figure A.3 provides some detail about how the Air Force responds at this point.[16] ACC and AF/A5XJ (the JACO) receive the RFF from USJFCOM through the logbook tasker, and it is also sent to AF/A3OO (the Air Force Operations Group).[17] AF/A5XJ uses the logbook tasker system to submit requests for information through USJFCOM back to the theater to clarify details of the RFF.

---

[14] ACC is the technical owner of requests, but it hands them over to A3O because that group is the functional owner (interviews with J3/JOD-GFM and AF/A4/A7Z personnel, December 6, 2007).

[15] For example, in the Army, the RFF goes to Army Forces Command and Headquarters, U.S. Department of the Army, at the same time. There are some units that Army Forces Command does not control, such as the medical unit and other direct reporting units. For the Marine Corps, Marine Forces Command runs the process.

[16] As of July 31, 2008, the process was under review as part of the revision of AFI 10-401, so this discussion is meant to provide a general sense of the Air Force process.

[17] According to interviews, ACC has effectively delegated management of the process to the Air Force Operations Group.

Figure A.3
Air Force Portion of the RFF Process

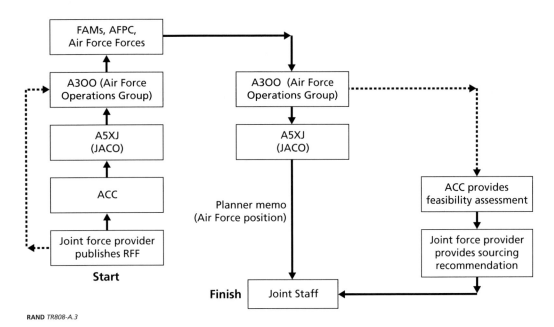

RAND *TR808-A.3*

AF/A3OO sends a "planner memo" to Headquarters U.S. Air Force, Air Force Forces (the appropriate staff supporting the COCOM), and major command FAMs; the AEF operations combat support division (AFPC/DPW);[18] and, if the tasking is for 365 days, a separate office in AFPC directing them to determine the feasibility of the Air Force fulfilling the RFF.[19]

The current operations branch of the Air Force Operations Group collects inputs from these organizations to develop a risk assessment associated with filling the RFF.[20] FAMs discuss with AFPC/DPW their ability to fill an RFF and the potential impact on UTC posturing (i.e., the readiness levels of UTCs that include personnel from their functional areas).[21] A3O-AOB chairs a weekly Air Force sourcing videoconference that includes ACC, AEF Center, AFPC, 2nd Air Force, AFCENT, and, occasionally, U.S. Air Forces in Europe, but most of the communication is by email.[22] All of these organizations consider Air Force and SecDef redlines as a risk measure to determine whether the Air Force can fill the RFF.[23]

---

[18] AFPC/DPW used to be called the AEF Center. In June 2008, AEF Center functions were placed under AFPC, and the organization's name was changed.

[19] 365-day joint sourcing solution assignments are managed by AFPC. Joint sourcing solution assignments of shorter durations are filled through the AEF assignment process. That is, they are filled by personnel who are in the deployment/on-call phase of the AEF cycle. See AFI 10-401, 2006, Figure 1.6

[20] AFI 10-401, 2006, Figure 1.4; AF/A5XJ, 2007.

[21] Air Force Operations Group–AEF Center meeting, March 5, 2008.

[22] Lt Col Laurel "Buff" Burkel, A3O-AOB, *A Proposal for Transfer of the Air Force Sourcing Process*, undated white paper, provided to the authors on November 12, 2007; JCS J3/JOD-GFM, 2007.

[23] Air Force redlines are violated if filling the RFF means that the Air Force's rotation policy as defined in Office of the Under Secretary of Defense for Personnel and Readiness, "Force Deployment Rules for OIF/OEF," memorandum, July 30, 2004, is exceeded; if the deployed to at-home ratio exceeds 1:2 for active-duty forces; if the RFF requires extensive training to assume noncore competency missions; or if filling the RFF requires changes to programmed unit conversion/deactivation/restationing plans. See AF/A4/7Z, 2007.

The FAMs determine whether the Air Force should submit a concur or nonconcur response to the RFF.[24] The decision is made with guidance from Air Force headquarters leadership and approval from the Chief of Staff of the Air Force; concurrence gives ACC approval to continue with the draft sourcing solution.[25] When there is a concur response, A3OB enters a spreadsheet attachment to the logbook tasker (as of November 2008, in JESS) that includes the Air Force risk assessment.[26] A3OO sends a concur memo through A5XJ to the Joint Staff, with a copy to ACC. A separate memo is also sent to A5XJ to ensure that the JACO signs the final review. Air Force guidance also requires ACC to forward a response to USJFCOM with sourcing risk and an Air Force planner memo.[27] According to our interviews, A3O and A5XJ coordinate throughout this process. Nonconcur responses are a rare occurrence and require general officer coordination and the signature of the FAM's functional commander.

From this point, USJFCOM makes its sourcing recommendation and forwards it to the Joint Staff. If there are nonconcur decisions (a service says that it cannot support the RFF) but USJFCOM determines that the nonconcurring service is the best solution, USJFCOM/J3 conducts a risk analysis of the solution. The Joint Staff business rules have guidelines for evaluating risk, and there is a list of GFM risk categories that are considered during the vetting process of the requests. The Guidance for Employment of Forces, which was still in draft as of July 2008, is used to prioritize allocation of forces.

USJFCOM provides its recommended sourcing solution and risk assessment to the Joint Staff J3/JOD-GFM, which can take three days to validate it, ensuring, for example, that something the Air Force will do matches the force tracking number from the COCOM. The sourced RFF package is simultaneously reviewed by the Office of the Under Secretary of Defense for Policy and the Joint Staff; the CJCS then makes a recommendation.

The RFF package is then integrated into the SDOB. Once a month, a senior officer from J3 briefs the SecDef on packages that are in the SDOB.[28] The validated sourcing solution is entered into the GFM allocation modification plan.

Filling ("Sourcing") the Request for Forces

In the execution phase, the Joint Staff (J3) writes orders based on the solution package, and the Joint Staff message center forwards the SecDef-approved deployment and execution orders to supporting COCOMs and services. If the Air Force is selected to fulfill the RFF, AF/A3OO notifies component headquarters to develop a formal description of the forces required[29] and

---

SecDef redlines are violated if filling the RFF leads to a deployed-to-home ratio greater than 1:1; if it would lead to more than 365 days of "boots on the ground" for active-duty personnel; or if filling the RFF makes reserve/guard unit reactivation necessary. See AF/A4/7Z, 2007.

[24] If there is a nonconcur response based on service redlines, this does not mean that the Joint Staff will not assign the position. Redlines are different for every service and are among the inputs that subordinate planners present to the SecDef on behalf of their service chief.

[25] AFI 10-401, 2006, para. 1.10.4.2.3.

[26] Discussions with AF/A4/7Z personnel, November 30, 2007.

[27] AFI 10-401, 2006, para. 1.10.4.2.2, Figure 3, and para. 1.10.4.1.6.

[28] If urgent RFFs arise, there can be a weekly SDOB. There can also be SDOB "special books" for RFFs that require immediate action.

[29] This is called "building the unit line number." A unit line number is a seven-character alphanumeric code that describes a unique increment of a unit deployment.

directs AFPC/DPW to source the requirements via an Air Force execution order. The order is transmitted by AF/A3OO to ACC, AEF Center, affected component headquarters or major commands, and the supporting AFFOR after the release of the SecDef-approved CJCS execution order modifications. For assignments that are for periods shorter than 365 days (most assignments are 179 days or fewer), AFPC/DPW tasks the major command that will support the requirement.

To fill the assignment, a UTC currently in the deployment/on-call phase of the AEF cycle is nominated by the AEF Center, and the major command validates that the UTC reports appropriately on whether it can or cannot fill requirements. The base then selects personnel according to who is slated for AEF deployment.

Joint Sourcing Forecast Model Methodology

Problem Overview

Military career field managers need to be able to manage and account for their personnel in support of DoD joint requirements. One of the problems career field managers face is the inability to predict future joint sourcing requirements and how those requirements might affect their future staffing.[1] The Joint Sourcing Forecast Model helps provide insight into future staffing conditions and show potential availability to fill joint sourcing requirements. It does this by showing month-by-month impacts on personnel caused by new recurring or nonrecurring ILO assignments, required deployment training, dwell times, accessions, separations, and nondeployable categories.

Layout of the Tool

Figure B.1 shows the main display for the forecasting model. From here, the user can manipulate various fields to see how changing factors, such as career field size, grade, deployment and dwell times, 179- or 365-day RFF requirements, percentage changes in accessions or separations due to the impact of previous deployments, analysis range, and so on, will affect the graph displays.

The bar chart at the lower left of the figure shows a breakout of all nondeployable categories, the total number of personnel deployed, and what we call the "naïve" deployment pool (what is left over after subtracting the nondeployable personnel and those already deployed from the total population). Each bar's height indicates the total number of personnel in the career field. The line graph on the lower right shows the total number of personnel deployed, the naïve deployable pool, and the actual deployable pool (the pool of personnel available for joint sourcing, taking into account dwell times and required deployment training).

Tool Overview

The top portion of the main graphical user interface (GUI) page (see Figure B.1) allows the user to manipulate career-specific values for career field size, current deployment and at-home dwell times, percentage changes in accessions or separations due to deployments, and selection

---

[1] Even the FAMs with whom we met who have a deep sense of their career field and "know" what will happen confirmed that this tool would be useful for communicating future impacts to others.

Figure B.1
Main Graphical User Interface Page

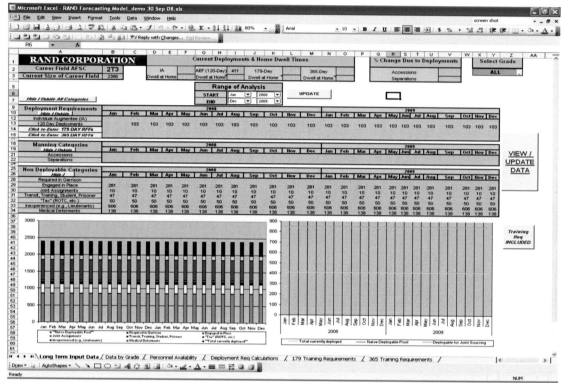

RAND TR808-B.1

of one or more grades to be analyzed. The tool also allows the user to specify the period for analysis out of a possible two-year maximum.

All data for the tool are entered by clicking the "View/Update Date" button on the main page (see Figure B.1). Clicking this button takes the user to the spreadsheets from which general or career-specific categories can be added or deleted, along with the associated data for these categories (see Figure B.2). The main GUI page includes the following sections.

"Deployment Requirements"

This section consists of requirements for individual augmentees and 120-day deployments, along with two buttons to enter new or changing RFFs. One button is for 179-day RFFs and the other is for 365-day RFFs. Data for 179-day and 365-day RFFs are input directly from the main page. When an RFF button is clicked, another spreadsheet pops up to allow the user to populate the following fields for the new (or revised) RFF: "Date of RFF," "Grade," "Length of Deployment," "Number of Personnel," "Date Required in Theater," "Required Training Time," and "Recurring Requirement (Y/N)." A recurring requirement is retained beyond the original term of the RFF. For example, if a 365-day requirement is recurring, the Air Force expects to fill that requirement every year. If it is nonrecurring, the requirement will be dropped after it has been filled for a year. This new information is automatically updated in the data and graph displays in the main GUI page when the RFF spreadsheet is closed.

Manning Categories

This section captures the career field accession and separation data. The effect of deployments on separations and accessions can be taken into account by entering a corresponding value (0–1) in the "% Change Due to Deployments" section at the top of the page. This allows a user to capture the impact of deployments on accessions and separations for the career field. This information is then reflected in the data and graphical displays automatically.

Nondeployable Categories

This section displays data for both general and career-specific categories. The general categories are as follows: "Required in Garrison," "Engaged in Place," "Joint Assignments," "Transit, Training, Student, Prisoner," "'TAX'" (nonaccession AFSCs), "Inexperienced" (e.g., lieutenants, junior airmen), and "Medical Deferments." The specific AFSC categories are defined and tailored by the user to enable a more specific career field analysis. The two graphs at the bottom of the GUI main page are based on the data in the "Non Deployable Categories" section.

Bar Graph

The bar graph at the bottom left of the main page shows a breakout of the total career field population. Segments of the bars show all nondeployable categories and the naïve deployable pool. This is the pool of personnel left when the nondeployable categories are removed (and includes those who are actually unavailable for deployment due to training or dwell times).

Line Graph

The line graph in the lower right of the main GUI page compares three lines for analysis. The aqua-colored line shows the number of personnel currently deployed, and the blue line shows the naïve deployable pool. The green line shows the actual number of personnel available for joint sourcing; this line takes into account dwell times and training times that limit the deployability of some personnel. The training that is needed for joint sourcing requirements can be included or not included in the graph by clicking the "Training Req" button to the right of the graph (see Figure B.1). If the button shows "Training Req Included," the tool takes into account the time that personnel will be unavailable because they are participating in training to prepare for their deployment. If it shows "Training Req Excluded," this period of unavailability is not taken into account.

Methodology

Underlying Data

The data underlying the model are contained in the "Data by Grade" tab of the spreadsheet (see Figure B.2). This tab can be accessed from the main GUI page by clicking the "View/ Update Data" button (see Figure B.1). This feature allows the user to input data by grade that the main screen will partially use as the back end for the analysis. The spreadsheet contains a number of preset categories that are standard to most career fields (e.g., "Accessions," "Separations," "Required in Garrison," "Engaged in Place"). The spreadsheet also allows the user to add or delete categories that are unique to a particular career field, providing the flexibility to create a customized tool to address specific concerns for individual career field analysis.

Figure B.2
Worksheet in the "Data by Grade" Tab

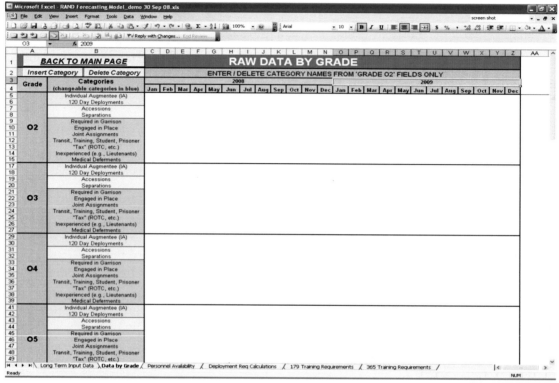

RAND *TR808-B.2*

Automatic Downloading of Data

The tool's structure is geared to enable automatic data download so as to avoid the time-consuming task of entering the data manually. The intent is that data for career fields will be pulled from government personnel databases in such a way that the resulting format is always the same. Once this process is in place, utilizing the tool's capabilities becomes much easier. The user will then be able to start the analysis with the base career field data already in place. This will allow the user to focus on tailoring the analysis toward career-specific issues and concerns instead of spending large amounts of time manually entering basic career field data.

Calculations

All calculations for the tool are done in the "Personnel Availability" sheet (see Figure B.3 for a sample). This sheet pulls in all data for computing the graphical displays and the monthly personnel data on the main GUI page (Figure B.1). The "Personnel Availability" sheet gets its data from several sources. These sources are the career field's data entered by clicking the "View/Update Data" button; the "179 Day RFFs" or "365 Day RFFs" buttons; and the "Current Deployments & Home Dwell Times," "% Change Due to Deployments," and "Select Grade" fields at the top of the main GUI page. The data are broken down by month and grade and are automatically updated when any of the inputs specified here are changed or deleted. The numbers of personnel currently on—or scheduled to be sent on—120-day, 179-day, or

365-day deployments, along with corresponding required training, are tracked month by month to determine when personnel become available for redeployment.

In Figure B.3, the numbers of personnel on 120-day, 179-day, and 365-day deployments are broken down to show which month of the deployment they are serving. The tool horizontally counts back the appropriate number of previous cells (months) to determine the current number of personnel deployed on tours of various lengths: four cells for 120 days, six cells for 179 days, and 12 cells for 365 days. Each of these deployment cells is also updated automatically as the vertical categories change (i.e., "Accessions," "Separations," "Career Field Total," "Emerging 120-day Requirements," "Emerging 179-day Requirements," "Emerging 365-day Requirements," "Required in Garrison," "Engaged in Place," "Joint Assignments"), with links to the user's inputs from the main GUI page and the "View/Update Data" sheet. This structure enables the tool's calculations to accurately and dynamically take into account all personnel changes in these categories while also adjusting for the month-by-month deployment fluctuations that occur as personnel return from, and leave for, deployments.

By taking into account those personnel who are available for redeployment, nondeployable categories, accessions, separations, and newly emerging ILO assignments, the graphs on the main GUI page show the overall picture of how the career field being analyzed is maintaining current requirement demands and help to highlight future personnel shortfalls.

Figure B.3
Worksheet in the "Personnel Availability" Tab

Microsoft Excel - RAND Forecasting Model_demo 30 Sep 08.xls

Raw Data

YEAR							2008										2009	
MONTH	Jan	Feb	Mar	Apr	May	Jun	Jul	Aug	Sep	Oct	Nov	Dec	Jan	Feb	Mar	Apr	May	Jun
Accessions																		
Separations	-65	-65	-65	-65	-65	-65	-65	-65	-65	-65	-65	-68						
Career Field Total	3171	3106	3041	2976	2911	2846	2781	2716	2651	2586	2521	2456	2388	2388	2388	2388	2388	2388
Emerging 120-day Requirements		103	103	103	103	103	103	103	103	103	103	103	103	103	103	103	103	103
Emerging 179-day Requirements																		
Emerging 365-day Requirements																		
Deployable for Joint Sourcing	1628	1563	1498	1432	1367	1302	1237	1172	1107	1042	977	912	844	844	844	844	844	844
Deployable for AEF	1628	1563	1498	1432	1367	1302	1237	1172	1107	1042	977	912	844	844	844	844	844	844
Naive Deployable Pool	1628	1563	1498	1432	1367	1302	1237	1172	1107	1042	977	912	844	844	844	844	844	844
Required in Garrison																		
Engaged in Place	281	281	281	281	281	281	281	281	281	281	281	281	281	281	281	281	281	281
Joint Assignments	10	10	10	10	10	10	10	10	10	10	10	10	10	10	10	10	10	10
Transit, Training, Student, Prisoner	47	47	47	47	47	47	47	47	47	47	47	47	47	47	47	47	47	47
"Tax" (ROTC, etc.)	50	50	50	50	50	50	50	50	50	50	50	50	50	50	50	50	50	50
Inexperienced (e.g., Lieutenants)	606	606	606	606	606	606	606	606	606	606	606	606	606	606	606	606	606	606
Medical Deferments	138	138	138	138	138	138	138	138	138	138	138	138	138	138	138	138	138	138
Total currently deployed	411	411	412	412	412	412	412	412	412	412	412	412	412	412	412	412	412	412
Undeployable because of Previous IA																		
Undeployable for AEF because of previous 120-day deployment		FALSE	FALSE	FALSE	FALSE	FALSE	FALSE	FALSE	FALSE	FALSE	FALSE	FALSE	FALSE	FALSE	FALSE	FALSE	FALSE	FALSE
Undeployable because of previous 179 ILO		FALSE	FALSE	FALSE	FALSE	FALSE	FALSE	FALSE	FALSE	FALSE	FALSE	FALSE	FALSE	FALSE	FALSE	FALSE	FALSE	FALSE
Undeployable because within 12 months of previous 365 ILO		FALSE	FALSE	FALSE	FALSE	FALSE	FALSE	FALSE	FALSE	FALSE	FALSE	FALSE	FALSE	FALSE	FALSE	FALSE	FALSE	FALSE
Unavailable Due to Training for Upcoming Deployment																		
Currently deployed as Individual Augmentee																		
Currently Deployed 120-day (or AEF)	411	411	412	412	412	412	412	412	412	412	412	412	412	412	412	412	412	412
Currently Deployed 179-day																		
Currently Deployed 365-day																		
120-Day Month 1	103	103	103	103	103	103	103	103	103	103	103	103	103	103	103	103	103	103
120-Day Month 2	103	103	103	103	103	103	103	103	103	103	103	103	103	103	103	103	103	103
120-Day Month 3	103	103	103	103	103	103	103	103	103	103	103	103	103	103	103	103	103	103
120-Day Month 4	103	103	103	103	103	103	103	103	103	103	103	103	103	103	103	103	103	103
179-Day Month 1																		
179-Day Month 2																		
179-Day Month 3																		
179-Day Month 4																		
179-Day Month 5																		
179-Day Month 6																		
365-Day Month 1																		

Long Term Input Data / Data by Grade \ **Personnel Availability** / Deployment Req Calculations / 179 Training Requirements / 365 Training Requirements /

RAND *TR808-B.3*

Entering a New Request for Forces

Figure B.4 shows how new RFF requirements are entered into the forecasting tool. When either the "Click to Enter 179-Day RFFs" or "Click to Enter 365-Day RFFs" button is clicked, the tool opens a new spreadsheet in which these data can be captured. The data fields are "RFF Number," "Date of RFF," "Grade," "Length of Deployment," "Number of Personnel," "Required in Theater," "Required Training Time," and "Recurring Requirement (Y/N)." When the spreadsheet is closed, the user has the option of saving the new data. If the data are saved, the tool will automatically update all related graphs and data fields.

Other Buttons

The main GUI page of the tool also provides buttons for additional functionality. Along with the "Select Grade" box, "View/Update Data" button, and "Training Req Included/Excluded" button, discussed earlier, there are the "Range of Analysis" and "Hide/Unhide" features. The "Range of Analysis" feature allows the user to select the range of months for analysis. To use this feature, the user would select a start and end month or year and then click the "Update" button. There are also "Hide/Unhide" buttons that can be used to hide one or more of the main sections ("Deployment Requirements," "Manning Categories," "Non Deployable Categories"). This feature is useful when the analysis of the career field includes a large number of

Figure B.4
Inputting a New RFF

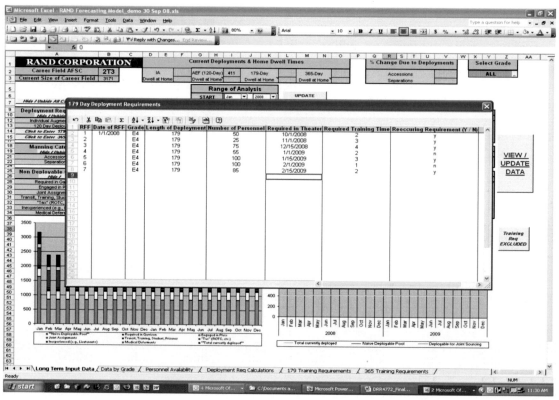

additional career-specific categories, causing the graphs to run off the screen. Using the "Hide/ Unhide" buttons will collapse the specified section(s). This allows the user to quickly view the analysis graphs after an update without having to continually scroll down for them.

Analysis Example

Suppose that a request for forces is received in May 2008 for 100 personnel to serve a 365-day tour starting in October 2008. Also suppose that three months of training will be required before the deployment. Figure B.5 displays the potential impact of accepting the RFF.

Notice that, starting in October 2008, the number of personnel deployed increases by 100 and the naïve deployable pool decreases by 100. Since this requirement was entered as "one time only," the number of deployed personnel decreases by 100 in October 2009. We have not yet included the three months of training required by these personnel prior to deployment. If this training requirement *is* taken into account (with the user pressing the "Training Req Excluded" button to change it to "Training Req Included," we have the display shown in Figure B.6.

Figure B.6 shows that, in July, August, and September (the three months of training before the actual deployment), the "deployable for joint sourcing" line is 100 personnel lower than the naïve deployable pool because the personnel to be deployed are in training. From October 2008 to October 2009, it appears that personnel are still available to deploy (the naïve deployable pool is larger than the number of personnel deployed), but potential dwell times have not been taken into account—there is no entry in cell I3 (next to "Dwell at Home" for AEF deployments).

Figure B.5
Initial Impact of a 365-Day RFF

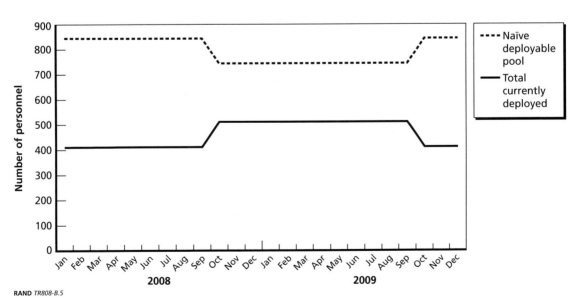

Figure B.6
Impact of RFF with Training Included

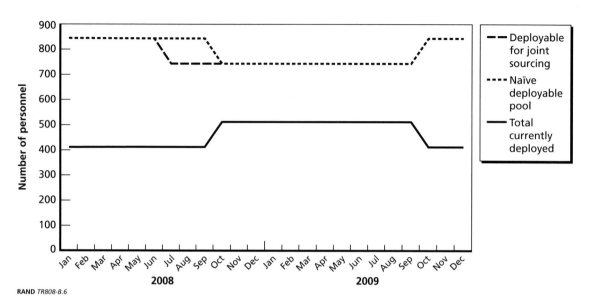

The value of this tool becomes apparent when we take into account the fact that personnel who return from deployment are generally nondeployable for a given period before their next deployment. For this example, we assume that this dwell time is four months for AEF deployments, so we enter "4" in cell I3. Figure B.7 shows the result.

The "naïve deployable pool" line is unchanged, but now the "deployable for joint sourcing" line appears and is dramatically different. In particular, we see that, from July 2008 until October 2009, the "deployable for joint sourcing" line drops below the "total currently deployed" line. When this happens, the tool turns the line red and displays a red "Personnel

Figure B.7
Impact of RFF with Dwell Time Included

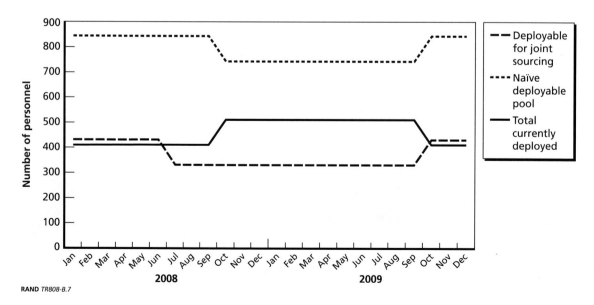

Shortage" block at the top of the page. From June through August, this shortage is aggravated because the personnel to be deployed are in their three-month predeployment training.

What this means is that, under the deployment policies entered by the user, starting in July 2008, there will not be enough personnel eligible to deploy for the number of required deployed positions if the RFF is accepted. One solution to this problem would be, of course, to argue that the Air Force cannot accept the RFF. Other responses could be to change dwell policies (for example, by decreasing the at-home time for AEF deployments from four months to two months in order to make more personnel available to deploy), to change policies governing other categories of nondeployable personnel, or to introduce policies that will increase accessions or decrease separations in order to make the available deployment pool larger.

The potential impact of these policy changes can be studied by making appropriate data entries in the model, and this capability is the model's most important contribution to personnel analysis.

References

2nd Air Force, "In-Lieu-Of Training," briefing, provided to the authors in October 2007a.

———, "In-Lieu-Of Training Concept of Operations (CONOPS)," draft, undated, provided to the authors in October 2007b.

AF/A5XJ—*see* Joint Chiefs of Staff and National Security Council Matters Division, Headquarters U.S. Air Force.

AFI—*see* Air Force Instruction.

Air Force Instruction 10-401, "Air Force Operations Planning and Execution," December 7, 2006.

Air Force Instruction 36-2101, "Classifying Military Personnel (Officer and Enlisted)," March 7, 2006.

Air Force Instruction 36-2110, "Personnel: Assignments," April 20, 2005.

Air Force Personnel Center, Interactive Demographic Analysis System (IDEAS), database. As of June 19, 2009:
http://w11.afpc.randolph.af.mil/vbin/broker8.exe?_program=ideas.IDEAS_Default.sas&_service=prod2pool3&_debug=0

Bailey, Kat, "Policy Changes Benefit Airmen Headed for 365-Day Deployments," Randolph Air Force Base, Tex.: Air Force Personnel Center Public Affairs, September 19, 2008. As of June 18, 2009:
http://www.afpc.randolph.af.mil/news/story.asp?id=123116124

Burkel, Lt Col Laurel "Buff," A3O-AOB, *A Proposal for Transfer of the Air Force Sourcing Process*, undated white paper, provided to the authors on November 12, 2007.

Conley, Raymond E., and Albert A. Robbert, *Air Force Officer Specialty Structure: Reviewing the Fundamentals*, Santa Monica, Calif.: RAND Corporation, TR-637-AF, 2009. As of January 18, 2010:
http://www.rand.org/pubs/technical_reports/TR637/

Defense Science Board Task Force, *Deployment of Members of the National Guard and Reserve in the Global War on Terrorism*, Washington, D.C.: Office of the Under Secretary of Defense for Acquisition, Technology, and Logistics, September 2007.

Ferriter, Michael, and Jay Burdon, "The Success of Global Force Management and Joint Force Providing," *Joint Force Quarterly*, No. 44, 1st Quarter 2007, pp. 44–46. As of June 17, 2009:
http://www.ndu.edu/inss/Press/jfq_pages/editions/i44/13.pdf

Gates, Robert M., "Utilization of the Total Force," memorandum, January 19, 2007.

Gibson, Brigadier General Marke F., "In-Lieu-of (ILO) Taskings," presentation to the Subcommittee on Readiness, Committee on Armed Services, U.S. House of Representatives, July 31, 2007.

JCS J3/JOD-GFM—*see* U.S. Joint Chiefs of Staff, Joint Operations Directorate, Global Force Management Division.

Joint Chiefs of Staff and National Security Council Matters Division, Headquarters U.S. Air Force (AF/A5XJ), "Joint Sourcing Primer," briefing provided to the authors on December 26, 2007.

O'Bryant, JoAnne, and Michael Waterhouse, *U.S. Forces in Iraq,* Washington, D.C.: Congressional Research Service, RS22449, updated July 24, 2008. As of June 19, 2009:
http://digital.library.unt.edu/govdocs/crs/permalink/meta-crs-10670:1

Office of the Under Secretary of Defense for Personnel and Readiness, "Global Force Management (GFM)," web page, undated. As of June 17, 2009:
https://www.mpm.osd.mil/owa/jrio/pkg_jrio.page?id=MP__GFM&wgsid=

———, "Force Deployment Rules for OIF/OEF," memorandum, July 30, 2004.

Schwartz, General Norton A., Air Force Chief of Staff, "Joint Expeditionary Tasking Term," memorandum, December 4, 2008.

Snyder, Don, Patrick Mills, Manuel Carrillo, and Adam C. Resnick, *Supporting Air and Space Expeditionary Forces: Capabilities and Sustainability of Air and Space Expeditionary Forces,* Santa Monica, Calif.: RAND Corporation, MG-303-AF, 2006. As of June 19, 2009:
http://www.rand.org/pubs/monographs/MG303/

U.S. Army, "Quartermaster Officer (92)," web page, undated. As of January 18, 2010:
http://www.goarmy.com/JobDetail.do?id=308

———, *2008 U.S. Army Posture Statement,* February 26, 2008. As of June 19, 2009:
http://www.army.mil/aps/08/

U.S. Army Installation Management Command, "History," web page, undated. As of January 18, 2010:
http://www.imcom.army.mil/hq/about/history/

U.S. Code, Title 10, Chapter 5, Sec. 153, Joint Chiefs of Staff, January 3, 2007.

U.S. Joint Chiefs of Staff, Joint Operations Directorate, Global Force Management Division (JCS J3/JOD-GFM), "Global Force Management," briefing, December 6, 2007.

War and Mobilization Planning Policy Division, Headquarters U.S. Air Force (AF/A5XW), "AEF Evolution: Tempo Bands," briefing provided to the authors on March 19, 2008.

Wynn, Michael W., Secretary of the Air Force, "Strategic Initiatives," presentation to the Armed Services Committee, U.S. House of Representatives, October 24, 2007.